The HANDMADE
BROOM

Create Your Own Designs from Scratch

The HANDMADE BROOM

Create Your Own Designs from Scratch

CYNTHIA MAIN

Text © 2024 by Blue Hills Press
Photographs © 2024 by Blue Hills Press

All rights reserved. No part of this book may be reproduced or transmitted in any form or by any means, electronic or mechanical, including photocopying, recording, or by any information storage and retrieval system, without written permission from the Publisher.

Publisher & Editor: Matthew Teague
Design: Lindsay Hess
Assistant Publisher: Josh Nava
Photography: Christina Stallard
Copy Editors: Chad McClung and Eric McIntyre
Index: Jay Kreider

Blue Hills Press
P.O. Box 239
Whites Creek, TN 37189

ISBN: 978-1-951217-54-9
e-book ISBN: 978-1-951217-55-6

Library of Congress Control Number: 2024940183
Printed in China
10 9 8 7 6 5 4 3 2 1

Note: The following list contains names used in *The Handmade Broom* that may be registered with the United States Copyright Office: Dexter; DMT; Ebay; Fiskars; Lie-Nielsen; Maine Thread; Makita; Mora; Morakniv; Gransfors Bruks; Greenlee; Silky

The information in this book is given in good faith; however, no warranty is given, nor are results guaranteed. Woodworking is inherently dangerous. Your safety is your responsibility. Neither Blue Hills Press nor the author assume any responsibility for any injuries or accidents.

To learn more about Blue Hills Press books, or to find a retailer near you, email info@bluehillspress.com or visit us at www.bluehillspress.com.

ACKNOWLEDGMENTS

To the team at Blue Hill Press: Thank you for putting your energy behind a book on broom making! The world gets a little better at craft with each book you release.

This book definitely would not have happened without the generosity of all the broom makers out there. For me, specifically, this means thanking Darold Francis, Gary Glascock, and all their teachers before them. A thanks also to Chris Robbins, Marybeth Garmoe, Hunter Elliott, and Erin Rouse for helping me pick up a thing or two along the way. I also have countless woodworking mentors to thank, but a special thank you to Drew Langsner, John Sarge, and Chuck Andrews for working with me on the hand tool side of learning.

And a technical thank you to Christina Stallard: This book would not be nearly as clear or as beautiful without your photos. Thank you Eric McIntyre for a final read through, and Jacob Goble: thanks, as always, for your excellent eye for design.

Thank you to the team here at Sunhouse Craft for weaving with me daily in the shop. I never imagined such a joy filled home for craft.

And huge thank you to my family, especially to my mom, Betty. Thanks for always encouraging me to follow my nose.

The time and space to write this also would not have been possible without the support and encouragement from Doug Stubbs: Thank you for being my partner in craft and in life—I am forever grateful.

CONTENTS

5   ACKNOWLEDGMENTS

8   INTRODUCTION

10 *Part 1:* **TOOLS AND SUPPLIES**

20 *Part 2:* **HAND BROOMS**

22   THE SETUP: HAND BROOMS

24   TURKEY WINGS

34   HAWKS TAILS

42   WHISKS AND POT SCRUBBERS

48   ROOSTER TAILS

58   WOVEN TOPS

68 Part 3: FLOOR BROOMS

140 Part 4: GOING DEEPER IN THE CRAFT

70 THE SETUP: FLOOR BROOMS	144 EXPLORING FIBERS
72 CREATING A HANDLE	146 DYEING BROOMCORN
84 COBWEBBERS	148 TOOLS FOR THE LONG HAUL
98 TRADITIONAL APPALACHIAN WITH BROOMCORN	
120 TRADITIONAL APPALACHIAN WITH JUST THE HURL	150 CLOSING
	150 RESOURCES
134 HEARTH SWEEPS	151 INDEX

INTRODUCTION

This is a love story. An obsession, really. Like many good love stories it all started with a chance encounter.

Back in 2013, after leaving my job running a teaching wood shop, I went for a year to Tillers International, a place to learn and practice traditional rural skills. I had always been working to stitch together my rural life and my life as a maker, and here was one of the only places in the country to learn traditional barrel making. It was a wood craft that totally fascinated me, and I was able to take a deep dive into the craft. It was there I had the chance to take a workshop on broom making from Darold Francis. I didn't realize at the time what was to happen from that first moment. Sure, it was a delightful craft, required only a simple setup, used natural materials, and had a beautiful and useful end result, but I couldn't have foreseen the sweet broom-making life that was about to open up before me.

After I left Tillers to open a small backyard cooperage with a friend, I kept making brooms. And making more of them. Soon a casual thing became an everyday affair. I was hooked, fascinated, obsessed. Brooms very soon took over the majority of my craft life. There was so much to explore within this simple craft, so much to do after learning the basics! After over a decade weaving, making thousands of brooms a year, I find myself still learning, still curious, still excited to explore what is possible within the bounds of this simple, but practical craft. I now find myself deep in the craft, with a broom shop and storefront in Berea, Kentucky, where I work hard to bring back the production of broomcorn to the region and help everyone catch the weaver fever that has changed the course of my life.

THE VISION

I've been wanting to put together a resource for people to start into the craft for many years: a how-to for learning the basic forms, some guidelines to start your own love affair. Call it a relationship guide, call it your trail map to connecting to land through craft. If you were not looking for a relationship, I am sorry in advance: that's always when the greatest ones appear in your life.

So come along as we learn the basics of Appalachian Style Broom Making. Some of my favorite things about it:
- → You need very little setup to make brooms.
- → You can grow your own materials.
- → You can make your own tools.

This book is divided into into four main sections: Tools you need to get started; a look at the canon of Appalachian style hand brooms; traditional techniques for making floor brooms; and a fourth section that builds on the foundation of the first three sections.

I highly encourage getting familiar with the basics, giving yourself a foundation to work off of, then using that as a launching pad to explore where you want to take the craft.

BUT WHAT ARE WE MAKING?

Appalachian style broom making is a regional style of broom making that typically has a very simple setup that can be done at home. These brooms are commonly made from a species of sorghum called broomcorn (the English used to call everything with a seed-head corn). Broomcorn moved into popularity somewhere in the 1700's, replacing the locally harvested sedges and twigs. While traditionally tied with hemp and wire, nylon was mostly used for binding brooms when I began learning the craft. We'll start with nylon, too, as we pick up the basics of broom making.

Hand brooms evolved into several distinct recognizable forms that include:
- → Turkey Wings
- → Hawks Tails
- → Whisks and Pot Scrubbers
- → Rooster Tails

Floor brooms can be divided into:
- → Cobwebbers
- → Traditional Appalachian 2 ways
- → Hearth sweeps

So let's get started.

Part 1

TOOLS AND MATERIALS

THE SETUP: TOOLS AND MATERIALS

Tools can be divided into four categories: what you need for handbrooms, what you need for floor brooms, what you need if you become a production broom maker (tools for the long haul), and tools for making handles, if you choose to finish them how I do. This section will cover tools to get you started in hand brooms and floor brooms!

Everyday broom-making tools: Clamp, stitching needle, my trusty awl, a broom-making knife, a tack hammer, and a set of Fiskars Pro shears.

THE HANDMADE BROOM

TOOLS AND MATERIALS

A SHARP KNIFE

We use knives in broom making for processing material, trimming broom corn, and slicing string. There is a traditional broom making knife that has a broad, flat side, as well as a sharp side. I honestly prefer two knifes: a wood carving knife (I use a knife from Morakniv, pictured) and a sawed-off cleaver handed down to me by Gary Glascock, who gave his equipment to me when he retired.

TOOLS FOR SHARPENING

It can feel like stepping off into the deep end, but sharpening doesn't have to be a mystery! You can skip ahead to the brooms, but we're opening with sharpening because it makes all the projects more joyful and less hard on the body. Granted, it did take me some time before I felt fairly confident with it, but, like most skills, practice will make it easier.

We're assuming you already have an established bevel and edge on your tool. This book will not cover how to reshape tool edges damaged by misuse. There's a lot to be said on sharpening. Some great resources for more information are listed in the appendix in the back, but a general outline of sharpening steps can be found on pages 14 and 15.

There are a lot of options for different sharpening stones. I personally use diamond stones. They are portable, and they stay flat, meaning you don't have to keep re-flattening your stone, which saves a step for sure! Diamond stones come in various grits (the lower the number, the more coarse the grit), usually labeled as extra coarse (roughly 220) coarse (320), fine (600), and extra fine (1200). You can also find sandpaper in these grits and attach it to a flat surface using spray adhesive.

LEFT: My sharpening setup: diamond stones of various grits and a homemade strop.

RIGHT: A traditional broom makers knife from Dexter, A sawed off kitchen cleaver (a personal favorite) and a small Morakniv knife. Many broom makers prefer the top one. I prefer to work with a combination of the bottom two.

DIY BREAKOUT
Sharpening

Sharpening is the process of bringing two planes together to meet perfectly. It happens by bringing an abrasive surface to the surface you are trying to sharpen and moving it back and forth in a steady manner. For the tools we are using in this book, you'll sharpen a single bevel, or slope, on each side of the tool. The cutting edge of the tool will be where the two sides meet, even if one is considered the "back". You will sharpen both sides of the tool.

Sharpening stones can be pricey, but it is worth the investment. Using dull tools can take a toll on your body and makes the work challenging and time consuming—if not impossible. One DIY solution is to get sandpaper in various grits—100, 220 ,320, 600, and 1200—and use spray adhesive to glue them to glass, which acts as a consistently flat surface. The sandpaper will wear out, but it is a way to get started!

If you are new to sharpening, you may find coloring the bevels of the tool with a permanent marker allows you to see where you are making contact with your abrasive surface, as the marker is removed in the sharpening process. If you are sharpening your tool for the first time, begin with the fine stone. If it seems like it will take forever to establish a sharp edge, go back to the extra course stone. You want to put the slope or bevel of the tool in full contact with the stone, always moving it so the sharp edge is not the leading edge (see photos at right).

Try to bring the bevel of the tool to the stone in an even, consistent manner. The stone and the tool must both be held steady to accomplish this, which might mean clamping your stone to a table or bracing it against something secure.

Apply a fair amount of pressure, continue to move the tool across the stone until you have created what is called a burr. A burr is a small wire edge of the metal that you have folded over to the other side of the tool. You can feel for it by running your finger towards the edge from the body of the tool (Not the other way! That's a good way to cut yourself!)

Lastly, move onto what is called a strop. This is usually a piece of leather glued to a flat board that has a small amount of honing compound applied to it in a diamond pattern. If there is buildup or too much used honing compound on your strop, gently remove it with your knife. Stropping acts as an extra fine polishing step and will leave your knife at a mirror finish.

TOOLS AND MATERIALS

1 Drag the bevel towards you on a stabilized diamond stone.

2 Repeat the process until you have a burr across the entire edge of the tool.

3 Flip the knife and register the blade so that the main part of the bevel is in contact with the stone. You will have to make a slight lift toward the end of the pass to make contact with the stone all the way to the tip of the blade. This will take some practice, so use a permanent marker to mark the edge of the blade to make sure you maintain the correct angle. And keep practicing. Drag the knife towards you with even pressure until you have rolled the burr back to the first side.

4 Repeat this process on each consecutive stone.

5 Apply honing compound in a diamond pattern to a clean strop.

6 For the final step, pull the tool across the strop evenly, keeping the bevel flat against the leather.

A FLOOR SPOOL

This acts as a spool of string that you control with your feet to create tension when tying brooms. For years I just used a stick, which I call a foot brake, and taught others to use a dowel. If you go this route, a stick that is strong and wide enough for your two feet and some thread are all you need for tying brooms! Should you decide to use a stick, I find it easiest to control barefoot. Some other options include a 2x4 with a rounded part in the middle for holding twine or a larger floor spool. This floor spool is made from two circles cut from wood mounted to an X made of wood and has a separate section for your twine and a section for your feet. I went straight from a stick to a tying table: If you plan to do any sort of production weaving, I highly recommend building a tying table (pictured below).

A SMALL AWL

Awls are essential for poking small thread ends where you want them to go.

BROOM STITCHING CLAMP

When we get to flat weaving brooms you will also want a broom stitching clamp. This tool mimics the action of a broom stitching vise, the more large scale setup.

NEEDLE & STAYS

You'll need a needle for stitching and two small stays to keep your flat weaving in place.

THREAD

I strongly suggest nylon for beginners. I know a lot of you will want to try natural fibers soon! Consider 2mm, 100lb test hemp when you do so. Natural fibers, with their different tendencies to break

TOP LEFT: A floor spool in the bottom of a tying table. Two crosspieces of wood to make an X shape to hold the spool (not pictured) makes for a more portable version.

BOTTOM LEFT: Easy at-home floor spools!

TOP RIGHT: Awls.

BOTTOM RIGHT: (top to bottom) A stitching clamp, 2 needles, and coat hangers for stays.

16 THE HANDMADE BROOM

TOOLS AND MATERIALS

DIY BREAKOUT
Make Your Own Tools

Having access to start a craft with very little startup cost is one of the great things about broom making! If you are just getting started, you can make your tools: cut a coat hanger to make the stays, file the teeth off a half a hacksaw blade and round the back to make a needle. Use a stick for a foot brake and any sharp knife will do the job. Some production broom makers prefer a serrated bread knife. Boom. You're ready to go!

Tools for the long haul will be covered in their own section towards the back of the book, so if you want to be able to weave for long stretches without adding injury to your body, look to the section called Tools for the Long Haul on pages 148–149.

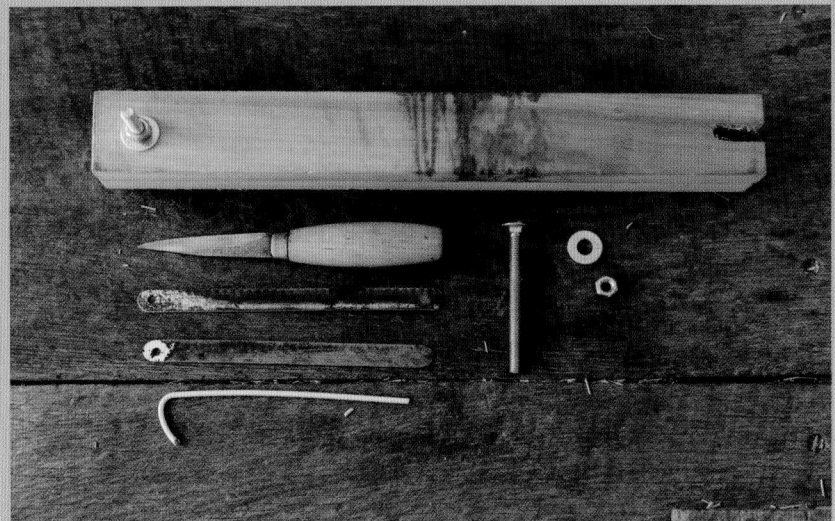

TOP: Handy shopmade tools include a clamp, knife, hacksaw blade needles, and a coat hanger stay.

BOTTOM: Filing down the teeth and rounding the front of a hacksaw blade to make a stitching needle.

THE HANDMADE BROOM

LEFT: Hot pink masonry line, blue and olive .040 diameter nylon string from Maine Thread, brown and tan 18# crochet nylon. Note the different gauges and names.

RIGHT: (Left to Right) Loose 18" hurl, craft broomcorn, unthreshed broomcorn from the field.

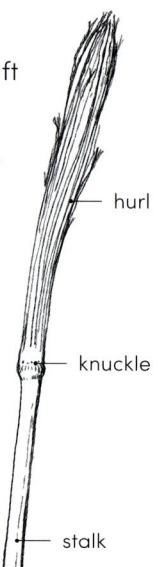
— hurl
— knuckle
— stalk

or stretch, add an additional layer of challenge to the broom making process that can make focusing on learning the techniques very difficult. Start with nylon, get the hang of it, and then you can add the complexities of natural fibers! To start with nylon, look for a 18# crochet nylon or a tarred 170lb. Test nylon: different makers will label it different ways. I personally love the 0.04" braided polyester (nylon) from Maine Thread Company. It's a bit finer, but I love their shop and the near matte vibrant colors.

BROOMCORN

Most makers start broom making by purchasing broomcorn ready to weave, so let's look at different parts of the broomcorn plant.

The stalk: This is the part attached to the root of the plant. Generally, by the time you work with it, this part is only 4-12" long, although the plant in the field usually stands 6-12' tall depending on the variety.

The knuckle: This is where the broomcorn splits into different sections.

The hurl: These are the loose fibers at the top of the plant you use to sweep with. If you're purchasing broomcorn, it is often sold as craft broomcorn, which includes the stalk attached for weaving, or as different lengths of loose hurl.

We go more in depth about sorting craft broomcorn for weaving in the Floor Brooms section on page 71. For the hand brooms in this section we will start with processed hurl. I demonstrate the hand brooms using 18" hurl, unless otherwise noted.

TOOLS AND MATERIALS

DIY BREAKOUT
Grow Your Own Broomcorn

You can definitely grow your own broomcorn! A variety of sorghum with a very long hurl, it is typically harvested right before the seeds mature. Check with a local grower in your area for help with this fairly easy crop to grow. If you grow on a larger scale, threshing, cutting, baling, and storing are another set of logistics to consider. Check the appendix in the back for more resources. If you are growing on a small scale, take into account that you'll need around 50 plans for a full sized sweep and plan your crop accordingly. You will want a way to thresh out the seeds if you go this route. A sawed off piece of an old handsaw, a curry comb, or mane comb all work well for threshing small amounts of broomcorn.

TOP: A field of broomcorn.

BOTTOM LEFT: Broomcorn plants harvested and ready for threshing.

BOTTOM RIGHT: Threshing broomcorn using a small mane comb.

THE HANDMADE BROOM

Part 2

HAND BROOMS

THE SETUP: HAND BROOMS

All the basic hand brooms we make in the first part of this book begin with the same setup, unless otherwise noted.

YOU WILL NEED:

→ A chair to sit in. I use a wooden chair; nothing on wheels!

→ Scissors, a sharp knife, or both.

→ A floor spool, or foot brake (aka a stick). This can be anything you can wind your string around and step on the sides of. Please note: Though not shown here, I tend to weave barefoot for better foot control.

→ A table or work surface in reaching distance is helpful, although not necessarily needed, especially if you feel comfortable working off the floor.

→ I also recommend having water or tea nearby!

NOTE: *timing*

After you start weaving, you really cannot get up until your project is complete. Try to give yourself an hour for each weaving project, though it will probably take less time.

22 THE HANDMADE BROOM

HAND BROOMS

DIY BREAKOUT

Tying the Jerk String and Winding the Foot Brake

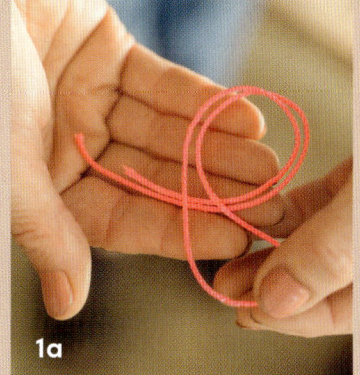
1a

1b

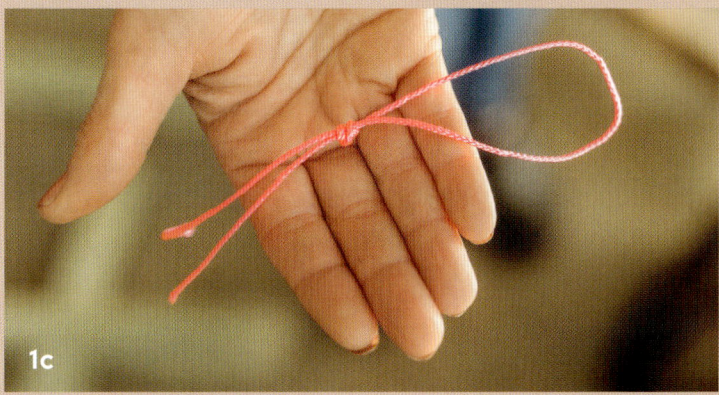
1c

A foot brake, or floor spool, and a jerk string are two things you will need set up for every project in this book. Let's cover the setup here, then jump into each broom project with these in hand.

1   A jerk string is a small loop you will use to tie off all of your projects. Traditionally they can be made with a wooden handle attached to the two "tails" of the loop as a pulling lever. Make a small loop in a line using an overhand knot. You should end up with an eye with two tails.

2   Tie your nylon twine to your spool or foot brake, using a small knot to hold it tight to the stick. Wind 80 times around your foot brake.

3   Tie a small overhand knot in the leading end of the line.

2a

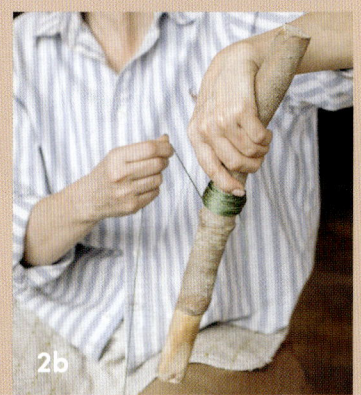
2b

3

THE HANDMADE BROOM

Hand Brooms

TURKEY WINGS

TOOLS & MATERIALS

→ 18" hurl broomcorn, a handful or 5 oz.

→ 18# crochet nylon

→ foot brake or floor spool

→ knife and/or scissors

→ an awl will be helpful, though not necessary

→ jerk string

Let's get started with the Turkey Wing. One of the most classic shapes when people think of Appalachian style hand brooms, this practical sweeper is great on floors when I don't want to get out the big brooms. This is a great portable project as well. After you get the hang of it, you will find you can make one in less than half an hour. So grab your foot brake and nylon cord, have a jerk string handy, and let's get started!

THE SETUP

Let's talk for a moment about the final shape we are looking for. In general, the shape if laying flat can be thought of as a triangle with a cylindrical handle coming off of it. The triangle is evenly fluffy across the sweeping edge of the broom. The evenness of the sweep is achieved mostly in the first step. Don't worry if the size of the bundles doesn't make sense at the first go at it. Just begin with what you've got and correct on the next one!

1   On a work surface, divide the broomcorn into 8 segments, laying them out in a cross pattern like the one pictured here. As you lay your bundles down, each bundle will be successively larger, until the final bundle you place on the stack is twice the size of the first one.

2   Have your foot brake or floor spool ready to go and your jerk string nearby (see page 23).

> **NOTE:** *bundle size*
>
> A note about the size of the bundles: If you want a broom that is evenly fluffy when you look from the working end, then you need to start your weaving with bundles that are BIGGER than the ones you finish with. It sounds a bit funny, but it is a great way to troubleshoot later. Take note of where your broom is sparse and add more broomcorn to that section on your next attempt!

HAND BROOMS: *TURKEY WINGS*

Now we are ready to make a broom! I usually use one of two ways to start. In the main text below, I walk through what I call the quick-start method. If you prefer a more classic approach, check out the box at the bottom of the page. Either method works fine—it's more a matter of personal preference.

LET'S WEAVE

3 Bury the knot on the leading end of the string from the foot brake in the middle of your largest bundle, keeping the foot brake under your feet, with very light tension on the line. Make sure this knot is firmly buried underneath where you will weave (pictured). This is the quick-start method I use that essentially ties itself into the broom as you go. If the knot hangs below where you weave, the whole broom could unravel.

A CLASSIC START

A more common setup that buries the knot ahead of time goes like this: Instead of burying the knot, pull 2" of thread through the broom, rotating your broom toward you until you have made a loop around the bundle towards the handle side of the broom, and just above where you pulled the thread through. Fold your loose tail up and against the broomcorn bundle and wrap another loop, this time with the tail below, locking the loose thread under itself. Then roll on to step 5!

THE HANDMADE BROOM

LET'S WEAVE (continued)

4   Wrapping always towards the handle end of your broom, wrap the nylon very lightly at first so as not to pull your knot loose. Wrap around the bundle three times, pulling very tightly on the third wrap. From here going forward, you will maintain this tight tension on the line for the rest of the process. You should be pulling with a lot of force, like picking up a small child. (Natural workout machine included!)

5   After wrapping around three times, you have a choice: Anchor the nylon twine near you with your thumb, allowing the twine to travel diagonally up one side of the broom before adding another bundle (5a), or wrap directly above the last wraps to make a close stair-step effect (5b-5c). You will then add the top bundle from your cross by sliding it in underneath the line until it sits neatly next to your first bundle, like you are adding pencils in a box. Please note: with the diagonal spacing technique, you'll add the bundle underneath (5a) while maintaining tension (with the solid weave directly in front). You will always be adding bundles in the same order, to the same place.

HAND BROOMS: *TURKEY WINGS*

NOTE: *claw and holding business*

When you add each bundle, you want to use your fingers in a claw-like motion, pinching your thumb and forefinger to each side of the added bundle to really keep that bundle from spreading out as you add tension. It is very common for beginners to have these bundles ooze out too much so you don't have a clearly defined stair pattern. Work on keeping each bundle shaped like adding pencils in a box as you continue to weave.

6 Continue adding bundles in the same manner until you have added all of your bundles.

7 You're getting close! Be sure to maintain your strong tension the whole time, and make sure your bundles are staying distinct. If this isn't happening for your first one, just keep going! Practice will correct many of the issues.

THE HANDMADE BROOM

LET'S WEAVE *(continued)*

8 Tip: Now you're ready to add a hanging loop! This method puts a small loop in the line, and with practice you can plan where it will land, but for this project, we will let it land where it does. This is the same process as tying a jerk string, just in-line. Tie a small loop in the line in front of the broom you are working on by about 4". You'll have to hold tension of the string with your thumb on the broom so the broom stays tight, release tension on the line in front of the broom, and use both hands to (awkwardly!) tie a small loop in the line in front of you that will soon be wound on to your broom. Return your tension to the foot brake.

9 Now add the jerk string. Lay your jerk string on your broom with the eye pointing toward the handle, and the knot below where you will wrap your final band.

HAND BROOMS: *TURKEY WINGS*

10   Continue wrapping the string with the same tension around the broom and jerk string, pulling very tightly.

NOTE: *don't give up*

If you have a disaster up until now, don't sweat it! Nail this next step and you can have a functional broom that can last a lifetime!

11   After 6 very tight wraps, with your hanging loop now on the broom, place your thumb tightly on the line, allowing the line to be cut while still holding everything tight.

12   Stab the loose end of string through the loop of the jerk string, then pull the tails of the jerk string firmly and quickly. Please note: this should be very hard to do.

THE HANDMADE BROOM

LET'S WEAVE (continued)

13 Grab the handbroom in both hands as pictured, and bend it hard over your knee—I always call this "shrimping" it, since I try and bend it to make a shrimp shape.

14 Trim the sweeping end with scissors. I like to leave as many of the fine ends as possible to catch more dirt. You can leave the handle side wild, or trim it with scissors for now. We will cover clean knife cuts in Pot Scrubbers and Whisks.

15 Your finished broom! The Fine Tuning sections at the end of each type of broom will give you tips on how to fix common problems as you go. It might take a bit before you are satisfied with your end result, so keep on weaving!

Celebrate! Really! Great job!

Now let's find ways to improve for next time:

→ Are the bundles evenly fluffy if viewed from the sweeping end? No? Adjust accordingly (see step 1 above).

→ Do your bundles appear distinct, or do they ooze around the broom a bit? If they aren't as distinct as you like, work on keeping them in a distinct pencil shape as you add each one—it's an odd combination of wrapping tightly and keeping each form.

→ Can you scoot the threads at all with your thumb? Yes? Then pull tighter! No scooting allowed! If you are having trouble pulling hard enough, but love everything else about it, you may want to skip ahead to Tools for the Long Haul and make yourself a tying table: It is MUCH easier to pull hard enough with a tying table.

Next time try adding a fiber loop handle. There are two main ways to add a handle: by tying a knot in the line as you go, shared in the step by step, or by inserting a separate loop handle underneath the final layers of wrapping. If you go this second route, make sure you wrap it underneath at least 5 or 6 layers at first. When your hand broom is complete, TRY and pull your handle off of your broom. Can you do it? If so, add more wraps, pull tighter, or add decorative little knots that hang out below the band to hold it tight.

FINE TUNING

Hand Brooms

HAWKS TAILS

TOOLS & MATERIALS

→ 18" hurl broomcorn

→ 18# crochet nylon

→ knife and/or scissors

→ an awl will be helpful, though not necessary

→ floor spool or foot brake

→ jerk string

Now that you are a broom maker, let's move on to the next traditional style of hand broom: The Hawks Tail!

It is very similar in setup to the Turkey Wing, but instead of adding all the bundles on one side of the broom, you will start with a central leader, and add bundles on each side of the broom. If you hold it up, it does indeed look like the tail of a hawk. Now, let's weave!

THE SETUP

I admit it, I weave a lot of Turkey Wings, but sometimes the work requires a broom that's spaced a bit more evenly in shape. Enter the Hawks Tail. I like this broom for more aggressive tasks like hearth sweeping. It's also a fun broom to make that builds easily on the skills you already learned.

1 Begin by grabbing a handful (5 oz. if you are the measuring type) of broomcorn. Divide the broomcorn into 7 bundles. This time you will make them bigger in sets of two. Lay down two bundles in a cross the same size, two more slightly bigger, then two more bigger than those. You will have one remaining bundle that should be about two times as big as the first ones you laid down.

2 Prep your string on your kick wheel or foot brake the same as you did for the Turkey Wing.

3 Have your jerk string, scissors, and/or knife nearby.

36 THE HANDMADE BROOM

HAND BROOMS: *HAWKS TAILS*

LET'S WEAVE

If you've been using a stick or foot brake and not a floor spool, you will probably find it easier to weave barefoot. Though I'm wearing shoes in the following photos, in reality I almost always weave barefoot and put my monkey toes to good use controlling the tension. If you've been having trouble with the stick kicking out from under you, go ahead and slide those shoes off!

4 Just like with the Turkey Wing, bury the knot in the middle of your largest bundle. Keep the foot brake under your feet and very light tension on the line.

5 Always wrapping towards the handle end of your broom, wrap the nylon from your foot brake around the bundle three times, pulling very tightly on the third wrap. From here you will always maintain this tight tension on the line.

To maintain this tension, you will have to let the foot brake "unspool" a bit. This is one of the reasons I like to work barefoot: Your monkey toes can help you maintain some tension while you allow more line to spool out, or you can hold your project with a thumb clamping the latest wrap, let off tension, then continue to weave. It is very easy, especially if you are a beginner, to end up hunched over to the ground. Try to find what is for you a comfortable weaving posture, and let the string off the brake to maintain that.

THE HANDMADE BROOM

LET'S WEAVE (continued)

6 Add the second bundle to the broom, pulling it up under the line, and in front of you. Make sure to keep it firm as one bundle. Use your "claw" grip to keep the broomcorn fibers together.

7 Rotate the broom a half turn so the bundle you just added is closest to you. Now add the third bundle. This is different from the Turkey Wing; instead of a full turn and add, you add on the half turn.

HAND BROOMS: *HAWKS TAILS*

8 Tightly wrap three times. Your nylon should be so tight it is essentially creasing the broomcorn.

9 Using your thumb-anchor technique you learned with the Turkey Wing, let the line spiral up a bit before adding the next two bundles in the same manner. How big of a spiral is a bit of an aesthetic decision, although the size of the bundles will force a certain amount of space to some degree.

THE HANDMADE BROOM

LET'S WEAVE (continued)

10 Wrap the handle as high as you would like. I like to think of how big the grip of the user is for my handles—usually in the 4-6" range.

11 Slide your jerk string in as you complete the first full rotation of the top band, with the "eye" up above the band. You want enough that you can thread the cord through, but not so much that it could fall out while you pull the tail of the jerk string.

12 Wrap 7 or 8 more times, secure the band with one final tug, and pinch the line with your thumb to hold the tension next to the jerk string on the same side your body is on. Cut the line, and thread the jerk string quickly. Then pull the jerk string through by pulling the tail, completing the broom. Cut the tail to ½" and tuck it in between the broomcorn fibers with your awl to hide it.

13 Celebrate the newest addition to your broom making family! We will cover getting a clean cut on the top in the next chapter.

HAND BROOMS: *HAWKS TAILS*

13

Now that you've added the Hawks Tail to your broom-making skills, let's look at some variations:

→ Is your broom evenly fluffy when viewed from the sweeping end? If not, adjust your bundles accordingly.
→ Play with the thickness of the bands and the spacing between them. It is possible to get a thick, stair-like pattern.
→ Experiment with handle length, placement, color, and sizes. I like to think of the final use and placement when considering these options.
→ Have fun exploring the endless possibilities!

FINE TUNING

Hand Brooms

WHISKS AND POT SCRUBBERS

TOOLS & MATERIALS

→ broomcorn hurl, possibly ends cut off from other projects

→ 18# crochet nylon

→ knife and/or scissors

→ an awl will be helpful, though not necessary

→ floor spool or foot brake

→ jerk string

Whisks and pot scrubbers are versatile little workhorses of the broom world. I love the whisk for sweeping popcorn crumbs out of my car. It also makes a great woodworking bench brush. Pot scrubbers are traditionally used for cleaning cast iron, or as cake testers—break off a sprig and insert it in the center of your cake like you would a toothpick. They also shine at hard scrubbing tasks, such as shovels or grills. I recommend hanging them to dry between uses.

WHISK

Often reserved for the longer sections of broomcorn too long to make floor sweeps, whisks and pot scrubbers can be tied several to a section or one at a time using scraps. In the steps that follow, I'm making a whisk and pot scrubber from a single bundle—a whisk at one end and a pot scrubber at the other. Once complete, simply cut them apart. The setup is the same as for the previous brushes.

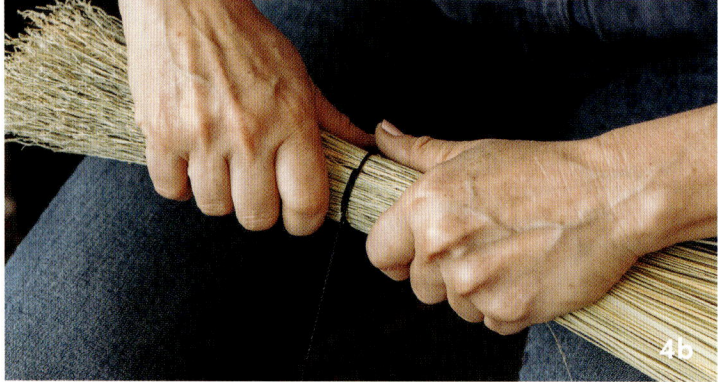

1 Select a slightly smaller handful (3-4 oz.) of broomcorn.

2 Have your jerk string ready, and floor spool or foot brake setup to start. See page 23 for a reminder.

3 Before you begin, tie a small loop in the line about 6"-10" from the end of your string. This will serve as a small hanging loop that you will work onto your broom in the weaving process.

4 Begin by burying the knot about a third of a way up the hurl, making sure the knot will be underneath where you are weaving. Add your jerk string as you complete your first rotation.

HAND BROOMS: *WHISKS AND POT SCRUBBERS*

5 Begin to wrap to make a band, only pulling tight after going around a few times, so the knot doesn't pull loose. At some point, the loop you made in the line will work its way onto the whisk. After you pass the loop one rotation, pull the knot out slightly so that the bands can nestle snugly together, leaving no space in the banding.

6 Wrap 6–12 times tightly, giving it an extra tug at the end of the wrap.

7 Anchor your thumb between your body and the jerk string and cut the cord, threading the loose end through the eye of the jerk string. Pull the tail of the jerk string firmly. This should be hard to do.

8 Cut the tail short, then tuck the remainder in with the awl.

THE HANDMADE BROOM

POT SCRUBBER

Now let's add a pot scrubber. I make my pot scrubbers 6" in overall length, with 1½" above the wrap, 1" for the wrap, and 3½" on the long side. To tie a whisk and pot scrubber on the same bundle I add the length of the end of the whisk to the long end of the pot scrubber, and start my bundle.

9 Begin by burying the knot in the broomcorn. Rotate the broom gently until you have completed one rotation. Add the jerk string in, eye towards the handle of the scrub.

10 Complete the band, anchoring your thumb before you cut and thread the jerk string as you did with the whisk. Pull the jerk string through. This should be hard to do.

HAND BROOMS: *WHISKS AND POT SCRUBBERS*

11 Cut the sections to separate into brushes. This should be fairly easy to do if you are cutting close to where you have a band. If you are having trouble, I also hear a ratcheting pipe cutter works. However, I really recommend taking some time and getting the hang of sharpening your knife, which will make the work fast, efficient, and satisfying.

12 Adjust errant ends into place using the flat side of a wide knife or by tapping on a flat surface.

13 Clean up with any final trimming using scissors or a knife.

THE HANDMADE BROOM   47

Hand Brooms

ROOSTER TAILS

TOOLS & MATERIALS

→ loose hurl: I prefer longer for this broom, while 18" will work, I use 20" in this demonstration

→ 18# crochet nylon

→ knife and/or scissors

→ an awl will be helpful, although not necessary

→ floor spool or foot brake

→ jerk string

I didn't learn Rooster Tails until very recently, and I have my friend Marybeth Garmoe of Ox-cart Broom & Woodworks to thank for showing me the way! I love the broommunity! If there is a traditional technique you are trying to learn, most broom makers are more than happy to show you! You will find this project much easier if you are proficient in making Turkey Wings, as it's basically a Turkey Wing with a flourish. If you find yourself still struggling after a dozen or so Rooster Tails, or not able to complete one, make sure you've really got a handle on Turkey Wings and try again.

THE SETUP

Rooster Tails are the peacocks of the traditional Appalachian shapes, fancy with a little bit of flourish. They might take a few attempts to make one you are happy with, but they are an eye-catching addition to your broom making repertoire. Functionally, they serve a lot of the same uses as the Turkey Wing; when a floor broom is just too big to get out, usually. I personally use them for my kitchen floors post cooking, or a quick sweep of the hearth or entry way.

1 Pull out about 4-5 oz. of broomcorn, or the amount you want to use in your broom. Note, I do this by feel and not by weight. For this one especially, although you will find it helps for any broom you are tying with nylon, soak your broomcorn for a count of 5 seconds in a 5 gallon bucket of water. Don't worry about soaking the working end of the fluff, just the part you will be manipulating during the weaving. If you find you are having trouble getting it to bend smoothly, give it another soak, or a heavy spritz with a spray bottle of water.

2 On a nearby working surface, divide the broomcorn into 8 segments. I like to use ones that are slightly smaller than a Turkey Wing, as they are easier to manipulate. Lay them out in a cross pattern like the one pictured here.

3 Have your floor spool and jerk string ready to start. For a reminder, please see page 23.

50   THE HANDMADE BROOM

HAND BROOMS: *ROOSTER TAILS*

Now we are ready to weave. We will go over the general motions of adding a bundle a few times, so hopefully by the end of the first one you make, the general motions will be clear.

LET'S WEAVE

4   Begin by burying the knot about ⅓ of the way up from the fluffy working end of the brush, making sure to bury it underneath where you will be weaving.

5   Rotating the bundle towards yourself, make a tight band of three wraps.

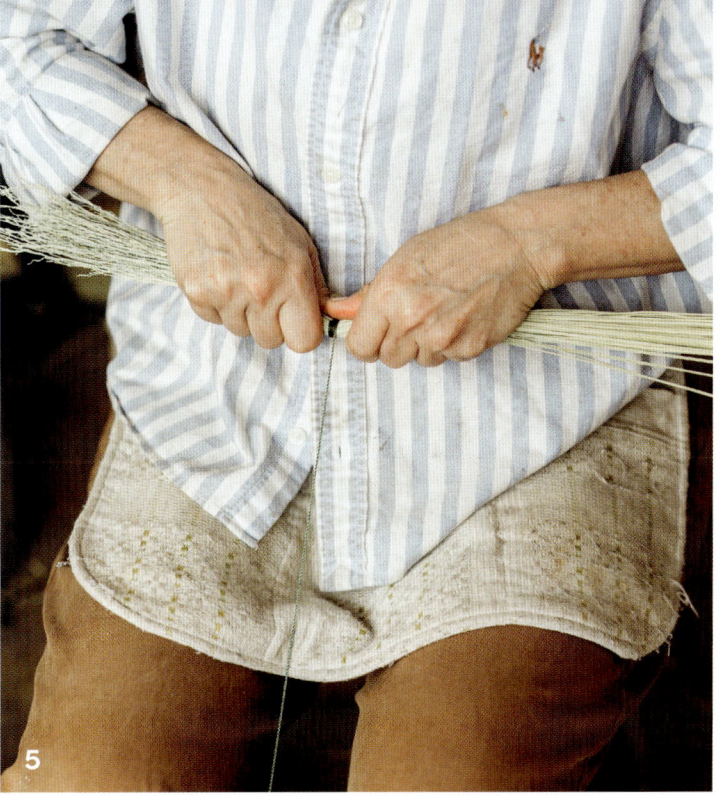

THE HANDMADE BROOM   51

LET'S WEAVE (continued)

6 Fold this bundle in half like you are closing a book and wrap another tight band of three around the little nub you have created at the end of the broom.

7 Open it back up as if nothing happened, nub side down.

8 Picking out 12 straws of broomcorn from the handle side, fold them down over the band you have just created, and split this group in half, pulling it neatly to both sides of the fluffy end of the broom.

HAND BROOMS: *ROOSTER TAILS*

9   Tuck your next bundle in on top of this pulled down section, but UNDER the line and begin to wrap. As you pass each side, pull up alongside the handle each small bundle of broomcorn, catching it under the string as you go.

10   Now you will repeat this process with each layer:

Pull out a small section of the handle, 12 or so straws, and fold it down over the last wrap. You have to sneak it under the current line you are working on.

Split that bundle in half and fold them down neatly along the sides of the fluffy end of the broom.

Sneak your next bundle of broomcorn under the line.

11   As you turn the broom to tighten this layer down, pull up each side you previously bent down, pinning it under the new row of string.

THE HANDMADE BROOM   53

LET'S WEAVE (continued)

As we continue weaving up the broom, let's review each step again.

12 Pull down a small section from the middle of the existing "handle" of the broom, and using your thumb to press it close, split the section in half to each side of the broom.

13 Use your non-dominant hand to neatly pull each section tightly and to the side.

14 Sneak your next bundle to add in under the line.

15 As you begin to rotate your broom, neatly pull each side segment upwards.

HAND BROOMS: *ROOSTER TAILS*

16 Continue to split down small segments from the center handle of the broom

17 Neatly press them to each side.

18 Add your next bundle in under the line.

NOTE: *style*

Where you place your bundles, how tightly you pull them will make a big difference in the overall appearance of the Rooster Tail when you are done. Keep this in mind, and take note of what you are doing as you go, and keep adjusting to the outcome you desire.

THE HANDMADE BROOM

LET'S WEAVE (continued)

19 Fold up the sides of the weave neatly.

20 Repeat until you reach the handle of the broom, and finish as desired. I personally spiraled all the way up the handle, then added my jerk string under a band at the top.

21 As you complete your first rotation of your top band, slide the jerk string in "eye" side towards the top of the handle. Wrap firmly pulling 6 or 7 additional times. Pull tension one final time, then, anchoring the tension with your thumb between your body and the jerk string, cut the line 2" in front of the jerk string, releasing tension from the foot brake, but holding tension with your thumb the whole time. Thread the jerk string, and quickly and firmly pull the tail of it. This should be hard to do.

HAND BROOMS: *ROOSTER TAILS*

22 Anchoring your broom on a firm work surface, neatly cut the top ¼–½" above the top band. Note, if you try to cut too far above, the broomcorn will move about as you try to cut it, giving an uneven finish.

23 Bend and scoot any of the bundles about as you check out your fancy new Rooster Tail.

24 Make your final cut of the end using sharp scissors. I like to leave as much of the split ends as possible for better sweeping ability.

FINE TUNING

As you begin to get the hang of the process, let's look at a few things to take note of:

→ Is your broom evenly fluffy across the sweeping end? If not, adjust your bundles accordingly.
→ Try using different size sections, both on the braid, and in general for each segment.
→ Think about loop handle placement, and handle length, and consider using some of the tools in the next section for a woven top on the broom.

Hand Brooms

WOVEN TOPS

TOOLS & MATERIALS

→ a previously woven broom of any type (Or weave one for this!)

→ stalks soaked in a bucket of warm water for at least 4 hours

→ knife and/or scissors

→ 18# crochet nylon

→ floor spool or foot brake

→ jerk string

Feeling extra fancy? Let's add a decorative woven top to the top of our hand brooms. A decorative handle gives a broom a great grip, and is a good opportunity to explore the wild world of patterns and colors. We will cover a plain weave, banding, and a twill pattern in this project. This project also takes a bit of planning ahead, so read through all the steps a day ahead of when you want to start, and plan accordingly.

THE SETUP

The variations are almost limitless after you get the hang of weaving. I look to a lot of basket makers and weavers for ideas and patterns. I also really love a neat, tight weave. A lot of the neatness of the weaving comes with selecting the pieces of stalk with which you will weave. I prefer to split them quite small, and make sure there are no general blemishes in the ones I am choosing to use. Take your time with the sorting and splitting section, and you will already have a leg up on the neatness of your weaving.

1 You will need to soak a large handful (20 or so) of stalks a few hours ahead of time in warm water. They have a tendency to float, so if you need to, you can weigh your stalks down with a weighted plate (not pictured).

2 Take each of your soaked stalks and split them in half. I stand them up on end for the first split, using my cleaver-type knife to split them down the center. I think it looks nicer if they are all similar in width, but to each their own. I split each of them to about a ¼" width, laying them flat on the table, and running my knife from the center to split them, discarding any that are too thin, have holes in them, or have weak spots that would lead to challenges later in the weaving process. The more neat and even at this stage, the more neat and even the weaving will look.

3   Tip: Want to neaten up the woven tops of your brooms? Go ahead and make a small bend in each piece about ½" down from the top. This will help you find where they nestle under the thread with more ease, and keep the visible outside of the stalk pieces from cracking from the bend. If any make a crunchy, cracking sound at this step, skip them! Chances are they will continue to crack through the weaving process, so better to weed them out of your pile now.

LET'S WEAVE

There are a few ways to start your woven top. You can either use the string that just wove the broom, continuing straight away into weaving the top, or you can loop around the broom a few times before you begin to add tension, crossing the thread over itself to lock it into place. I like to add the thread to the bottom of where I will be finishing the woven top, then spiraling up to the top to start, as seen in picture 1.

1 Make the first band where you would like the woven top to attach to the broom.

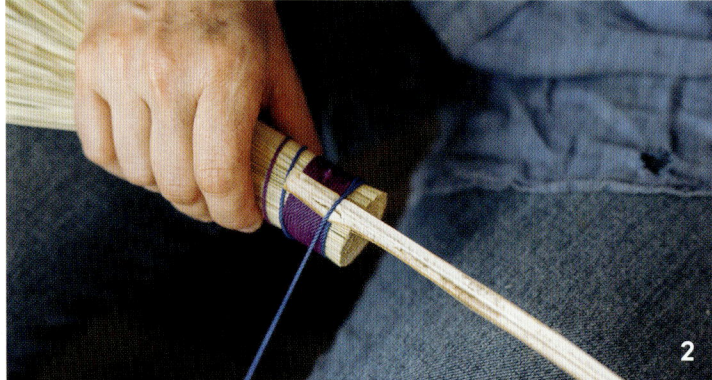

2 After you have a tight band, begin one by one adding your stalks upside-down, and with the long part hanging off the top of the broom. We will fold them all down after a full circle has been added.

3 After making a complete rotation adding each piece, make another rotation of the twine for extra security, then spiral down about ¼-½".

NOTE: *pattern consideration*

If you want the classic over-under pattern to work out, you will want an odd number of reeds. Full disclosure: I don't count. I simply add what fits, then begin weaving. If I have the wrong number for the pattern to work out, I simply go back to where there is one reed that is a bit fatter than the rest, split it in half, and keep going. If you are a planner, plan, or know there's a backup if it doesn't work out.

HAND BROOMS: *WOVEN TOPS*

4 Trim down the stalks that are exceptionally long. You really do want to keep as much length as possible for the weaving process, so rather than trimming them all to the same length, just top the super long ones.

5 Sliding your hand behind the stalks, gently fold them down over the top nylon band.

6 Make a band by continuing to rotate the broom three more times.

7 When you are at the same spot that you started, using your thumb at the base of the reed, gently lift a stalk SIDEWAYS at the same time you swoop the broom. This allows the line to easily pass underneath the stalk. Each time you pass a stalk, there is a slight tug you do to nestle the string as close to the last row as possible. The whole motion is a flip, a swoop of the brush, and a cinching down.

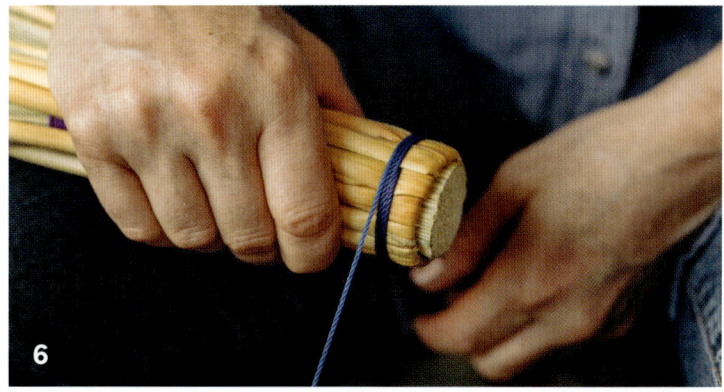

THE HANDMADE BROOM 63

LET'S WEAVE (continued)

8 The string will go where it wants to if you don't take a moment to tell it where to go with a light cinching motion. Always tighten the string down where YOU want it to go. Sometimes this will involve wiggling the stalk like a loose tooth to make sure the string slides all the way up to where you want it to be.

9 Wrap over the next stalk in order. Go under, and continue the pattern until you have gone all the way around.

10 When you arrive where you began to weave, you should be going over the stalk you previously went under. Always use that same sequence of lift, swoop, cinch. If the pattern didn't work out, split a large stalk carefully to create two weaving elements, then continue weaving. After you have gotten the hang of this pattern, make a small band three rotations tall on your handle, then let's practice a twilling pattern.

NOTE: *twilling*

I learned twilling by asking the weaver Emilie Weber Wade to help me learn some new patterns. I was terrible at it at first. Even though it was so similar, I had made the same pattern for so long, I found it so challenging for my brain! If you have the right number of stalks for over/under to work out, the twilling will work out great! You will have an overlap of one stalk as you go, making a tiny stair step pattern.

HAND BROOMS: *WOVEN TOPS*

11 For the twilling pattern, I begin by making a band to set it apart from the plain weave. After the band is made, switch to over two, under two to create the twilling pattern, giving the same attention to keeping the pattern tight. It should begin to make a stair-like pattern as you progress. Finish off your twilling section with a tight band of two times around the broom.

12 To make a space between this band and the final band, carefully sneak the cord behind all the stalks, spiraling ½" towards the end of the broom, making a complete rotation BEHIND all of them. This is just a sneaky way to make two bands with no obvious connection. Pop back out to begin your final band.

13 Add your jerk string in with the "eye" of the jerk string on the sweeping end of the hand broom as you finish the first full wrap of the band. Cut the line, hold tension as before, and pull your jerk string back up towards the top of the woven handle.

14 Using an awl, tuck the loose end of the tail under a weave.

THE HANDMADE BROOM

LET'S WEAVE *(continued)*

15 Gently cut through the stalks in an even band if you so desire, minding to not cut the fibers below.

16 You did it! There are so many possibilities for woven tops. Look to any woven patterns as sources of inspiration to take your weaving further!

FINE TUNING

→ Let's look at the weaving you did. Are you pleased with how it came out? What changes do you want to make?

→ If you want to weave tighter, it is usually a matter of TELLING the string where you want it to go with tiny motions: Angle the broom so the layers stay tight, and be gentle and support the base of the stalks if they are tearing.

→ Please remember it takes practice to get a neat, tight weave. Enjoy the journey!

HAND BROOMS: *WOVEN TOPS*

THE HANDMADE BROOM

Part 3

FLOOR BROOMS

THE SETUP: FLOOR BROOMS

This next section covers brooms with handles, and is split into brooms where the stalk is attached and woven, and brooms where the hurl is attached to the stick with a decorative cap woven over top. Last, we cover variations on smaller brooms with handles also called hearth brooms.

These big brooms are really the reason broom making stuck for me. A well-made broom is so ergonomically wonderful to use and so good at sweeping due to the split ends of the broomcorn, it really is something to experience. After I made my first one, I was hooked on the feeling of using them as much as the joy of making them.

Making a broom happens in a few steps: sorting and soaking the broomcorn, preparing the handle, weaving the head of the broom, then flat or round stitching the broom.

SORTING BROOMCORN

We will start with what is called craft broomcorn, or broomcorn with part of the stalk below the knuckle still attached. Craft broomcorn usually comes in a large bundle, if you do not grow it yourself, and has various lengths of hurl above the knuckle. Before I make any brooms out of it, I like to sort it into the right lengths that will work best for different projects.

SORT AND SOAK THE BROOMCORN

One of the great things about making your own Appalachian style sweeper is you can leave all the small, curly fibers at the top of the plant. These do a wonderful job of sweeping, as opposed to the blunt cut (great for patios and stone!) that most commercial brooms have. How you get those ends into a broom involves sorting your broomcorn before you start working with it. I was taught to sort it into 2" increments: 14" of hurl, 16", 18" and so on up to 24" and above. Note: A lot of commercial, readily available broomcorn seems like the hurl has gotten longer the last few years, so you may find yourself making a larger sweep to accommodate the length of the broomcorn.

The 16" and 18" make wonderful full sweeps. The 20–22" make great cobwebber brooms and full sweeps that will get a flat cut. I save the stalks with really long hurl to make whisks and several pot scrubbers, cutting off the stalks for decorative weaving later.

After my piles are sorted, I bundle them and put them back on the shelves.

Do I always do this? No. Can I tell by the feel of picking it up how long it is? Yes! These days, I skip anything over 20" going into my soaking bucket (more on soaking soon!). This means some of the ends will be trimmed but most will stay long.

If you are tempted to skip this step, I highly recommend trying it once, making a sweep of even length broomcorn hurl, and sweeping with it. It just might win you over!

Now that the broomcorn is sorted, let's start by soaking some of the 22" broomcorn to make a wispy cobweb-sweeping broom. Take 25 stalks and make a bundle, loosely tying them halfway up the bundle so the water can penetrate all of the stalks. Submerge the stalks to just past the knuckle in a 5 gallon bucket of warm water. It usually takes a pretty full bucket to do so. If you have any stalks over 8" in length, now is a great time to trim them down so they are fully submerged in the bucket. We will leave that to soak for about 4 hours while we go get handles and prepare them for the weaving process. If you are new to preparing handles, you may want to soak the broomcorn AFTER the handle is ready.

Soaked craft broomcorn. Note how the plant has been soaked to just past the knuckle.

CREATING A HANDLE

This section is on finding good handles for your brooms. There are several ways to go about this, but I prefer to get our handles from downed branches from the woods here in Berea, Kentucky. I do this for a few reasons:

- → It's a great excuse to get outside and be in the woods! (Although no excuse is needed.)

- → I can find specific shapes, with specific people in mind. I make each Appalachian style sweeper to order. With the user in mind, I head to the woods looking for specific sticks that I think will best suit.

- → I can shave off the bark (or kiln dry it!) and not worry about sending borers or bugs across the country.

- → Special features, such as the unique quality of wood that could be spalted from spending time on the forest floor, give the broom a singly beautiful nature that I love.

It's good to know at this point that you can also purchase handles that are ready to go from different suppliers: dowels, tobacco stakes, and kiln dried handles can be put to good use here. I was also taught that willow and sassafrass are good, traditional handles. Establishing a place where you can coppice these is another great long-term strategy. For more information on Coppicing see the Appendix at the back of the book.

One of the most delightful parts of broom making, I love gathering handles from the nearby woods.

NOTE: *why dry the handles?*

Drying the handles, or removing the bark are both ways to prevent spreading nasty intruders like the Emerald Ash Borer. I personally don't want to be responsible for wiping out entire forests, so I take this part seriously. Setting up a small kiln (solar or otherwise) where you bring the sticks to 140° farenheit for a period of time, at least an hour, also works. I encourage you to check in with someone from your local forest service if you want to learn the dos and don'ts of moving wood in your area. It is a serious matter, and carelessness has led to the destruction of many a forest!

Let's head to the woods! I bring with me my folding saw, I use a small Silky. I like that it is orange so I can find it in the woods, and it has a good blade, which to me is one that can do the work with minimal physical effort. This saw cuts on the pull motion, meaning I only apply pressure on it while I pull it towards me.

I look for branches that I think will shave down to about 1"- 1½" in final diameter. When I find one I like, I smack it against the ground HARD! Did it break? No? It's a keeper! Yes? Then sadly, leave it there on the forest floor. I have been known to, on occasion, take home a brittle stick as it was too pretty to pass up, weave a broom head on it, and have the whole head break off from the weight of it.

After I find a stick I love, I saw it off at hip height. This should give me plenty

Use good form to cut a handle to length safely.

of room to cut it to the right length after shaving it down in the shop.

If I am cobwebber stick hunting, handle length really depends on the height of the ceiling. I personally like really long and skinny sticks to reach high ceilings. After I have the sticks gathered that I need, I'll head back to the broom shop.

At this point, you can either kiln dry your wood to kill borers, or remove the bark.

I'll go over some simple kiln options first, then go more in depth on how I remove the bark using green woodworking tools.

KILN DRY IT

Full disclosure, I don't have one, but here's the deal: bringing wood up to a temperature of 140° farenheit for an hour should kill all bugs. (There is a LOT of chatter and debate on this, some say 133° for the entire piece of wood for any amount of time, some say 130°. I go with 140° for an hour to be safe).

> **NOTE:** *falling for pretty sticks*
>
> A word of warning about falling for cute sticks in the woods: One of the great things about this craft is getting to use things that grow right there. When you start really LOOKING at sticks, you will find there are some, like a siren calling from the rocks, that are hard to say no to. I wish you luck as you get seduced by crumbly wood, rotten limbs, and skinny sticks. I too, fall for their beauty on occasion. If you want to make a very practical sweeper, though, stick to the ones that are straight as you can find (here's where coppicing would really shine) and sturdy, without too many knots.
>
> If you are looking for a wild time, go bananas, just try and stick to things that will hold up through the weaving process. And a word of note: The counterbalance as you weave on a really curvy or top-heavy stick will make weaving much harder!

CREATING A HANDLE (continued)

Woodworking is one of those spots where folks love to debate best use, so pick your favorite expert (I went with our local forester), and build something accordingly. A link to good plans for kiln options can be found in the Appendix.

I choose the remove-the-bark method to make sure I don't send borers across the country. It ties in my love for green woodworking to the craft. When I first learned the craft, we used sanders to remove the bark, and a Polyurethane/shellac to finish them. If that is your thing, go for it! In this book, we will use my favorite tools instead.

Now that we are headed for removing the bark, let's back up a second to do a crash course in green woodworking. You do not need any experience to hop in on the fun of green woodworking, but you will need some specialized tools. In each section, I've included my favorites, as well as a price typical range. I built out my tool collection over the years and can remember not too terribly long ago when even buying a knife was a major decision. Work with what you have, keep looking for what you don't, and build your tool collection as you can.

ANIMAL, VEGETABLE, MINERAL

While taking a class to improve my axe work with Drew Langsner, who previously ran Country Workshops in the mountains of North Carolina, he shared the idea that green woodworking is the meeting of animal, vegetable and mineral. You're the animal, the material you're working with is the vegetable and your tool is the mineral. Anything is achievable if all those things are in balance: the right tool, the right wood selection, and the right technique. If one of those elements is lacking, then you may not be able to achieve what you are trying to do. Consider it part of the learning process as you develop a knowledge bank that helps you achieve what previously was not possible for you.

SOME GENERAL THINGS TO NOTE

Branches/trees/wood all have what is called grain. You can think of it like the direction of growth–like hairs on a cat, they are nice to pet in one direction, but it doesn't go so well in the other (ask any cat! You can thank Mr. Langsner for the analogy). Unlike a cat though, grain direction can shift in a piece depending on what the tree was trying to accomplish in that space.

A general rule is that a tree's grain is moving to support its limbs. If you come to a knot in the wood (where a branch was or was going to be), approach the knot from both sides with the tool, as a starting place. This is a very general truism, but you can think of it this way: You can have some sticks with grain going in one direction generally, and towards the knots at those places, while others will switch grain direction ALL THE TIME. As you become more familiar with different species, their behaviors, and most importantly, the feeling of the tool when the grain shifts under it, adjusting how you are working with the tools will become second nature.

We'll use this basic principle to generally use our tools in the direction of the grain to give a smooth finish and prevent tear out (when the wood chips out and leaves rough holes in your work). You will see this come up in each of the phases below. If you notice this, you can usually tell that they are tearing in one direction. Try using your tools to approach the work the opposite way over this section of the branch.

Another thing to keep in mind is that, based on the species of harvest, the time of year, and the age of the wood, the bark will be easier or less easy to remove from the branch. If you are finding it too difficult and you know your tools are sharp, you may want to take note of these factors. Talk to knowledgeable folks in your area about species that grow there and pass on a particularly challenging stick.

It's also very true that if your tools are not sharp enough, you will encounter more and more of these problems. A very sharp tool used correctly can smoothly and easily cut through most situations you encounter when cleaning sticks this way. We'll cover sharpening as we introduce each tool in the process.

Please also be kind to yourself as you learn! Woodworking is something that improves with time and experience. Now that we have the internet, it's so easy to watch experts with years of experience execute nearly flawless snippets for us to see. Remember to keep practicing, enjoy the learning curve, and sharpen your tool!

GREMLINS! (DON'T FEED THEM AFTER MIDNIGHT!)

If you're old enough to remember *Gremlins*, the movie, you may remember that those cute little Mogwai came with a few rules. Break them, and the outcome can be very bad. The same is true for working with sharp tools!

Here are some rules that I apply to working with sharp tools:

→ Don't work when you are tired.
→ Don't work when you are angry or too emotionally overwhelmed to concentrate.
→ Wear appropriate clothing.

My set of handle-shaping tools: A Silky handwsaw, a Gransfors Bruks axe, Lie Nielsen spokeshave, and a Greenlee drawknife. Fancy, I know.

CREATING A HANDLE (continued)

These are all the situations I avoid, as they are when I've seen most injuries happen. I've never given myself a major cut and plan to keep it that way. You know yourself. Add your own rules to this list and stick to them! Get a buddy to stop you if they see you cursing and headed for the wood shop. My personal list also includes no major decisions after 4 o'clock in the afternoon. Your current and future fingers and toes will thank you!

> **NOTE:** *disclaimer*
> This book covers how I do things. If the instructions don't feel clear, get help from me via email, or from another more experienced practitioner. Safety notes will be part of each tool introduction.

AXE

Generally, in green woodworking, use the biggest tool you can to do the most work before moving onto the next, smaller tool. It saves time, creates efficiency, and prevents injury to the body. You can spend all day using a knife to clean up a knot, or you can saw it pretty clean, and use an axe to remove it in two chops. So we'll start in the shop, after sawing off any major branches of our stick, by using the axe.

Picking an axe for carving:
I'm a relatively small person with fairly small, some might even say child-sized hands. So these are what work well for me, which generally means the lighter and smaller options. Some axes I use are:
- → A small Gransfors Bruks Axe
- → A Kathoff Axe
- → A Fiskars Axe. I tried all the readily available hardware store axes, and honestly, this one was a clear winner. If you're on a budget, it's a decent option.

Before I had the money to purchase any of these, I just used a random garage sale hatchet that I sharpened. It's a fine option and shouldn't run you any more than $20. A new handmade axe can cost up to $300.

A Kathoff axe and a Gransfors Bruks axe. Both fancy options that work wonderfully. I use them both for different purpose.

> **NOTE:** *Choosing and using an axe— take a class!*
> When I first wanted to get into this, I went and took a class with the legendary (at least to me!) Drew Langsner becauseI couldn't find anyone around me with good axe knowledge. I had read all the books I could find, but wanted to learn more. (This was pre internet, y'all....there was a time before YouTube took off...!) It was a great experience, and while the internet has bloomed with lots of options since then, I highly recommend taking a class in person if you can. The amount you can learn in a short time is astonishing!

DIY BREAKOUT
Sharpening an Axe

We are going to go back to the same basics of sharpening that will come up over and over again in this book. You always want to create a situation where you're bringing a steady stone to a steady tool at a consistent angle. This is going to take a little practice. Don't be afraid to go slow, mess up, and try again later. I spent the better part of a year going from horrible to very proficient. Just keep practicing and improvement will come.

Find a way to hold the tool in a steady spot. I generally use two clamps to clamp the axe to the corner of a table. Color the blade with a permanent marker so you can see when you are where you want to be with the stone.

In general, you want the stone to make contact either in the center of the marker-covered section, or wherever you can visually see that the edge of the blade you are sharpening has a spot that sticks out higher than the rest of the blade. You want to find a way to hold your angle consistently as you move your stone across the tool. Even though the axe has a curved blade, it's generally the same plane all the way across the blade. Sharpen until you have raised a small burr across the entire edge, as you did with knife sharpening. Flip, repeat, and move up the grits as before. If you need a refresher on the general principals of sharpening, head back to pages 13–15.

Now that you have a sharp axe, let's get to work! People often ask, "But when do I sharpen it?" My answer is: when the blade is noticeably not as sharp as when you first started, or when you cannot accomplish what should be easy. Sharpening more frequently actually prevents spending a longer time going back to coarser grits and saves wear on your body as well.

Firmly anchor your axe and hold your stone in a way that you can bring it in consistent and steady contact with the axe blade. Move across the entire surface until you have raised a burr over the entire edge. Flip, clamp, and repeat. Steady as she goes!

CREATING A HANDLE (continued)

TOP: Using an axe to take down knots.

BOTTOM: Sitting at my shaving mule ready to go (note the diagonal hand position).

The axe will be used in combination with a chopping stump. This is a very large, sturdy stump that will act as an anchor for your work. Please use something stable as a surface to help prevent injury.

We will begin by working to axe off any big knots or bulges on the wood. Use your dominant hand to hold the axe in a choked-up manner. With your other hand, especially when you are first starting out, keep the hand that is holding the stick above the ENTIRE swing range of the axe. There should be no possibility of you hitting any part of that hand. A general rule of thumb is to approach the knots from both sides. Think of a knot as the stump of a branch, like where your arm comes out of your body. The fibers grow towards that in both directions to support the branch, so approach each knot with a light swing. Then when you have chopped halfway through the knot, turn the stick over and come at it from the other side.

When you're first learning to do this, the tendency will be to overgrip, use too much force, and lack a precise aim. Think of relaxing your body as you lightly swing, allowing the natural rebound to help you stay relaxed. Let your sharp tool do the work for you.

Repeat the process with any knots on the handle.

Now that we've leveled off any major knots or branch starts, we will move to the next pair of tools: a shaving mule and drawknife.

HORSES, DONKEYS, AND MULES

There are LOTS of types of shaving horses, or fancy foot-powered clamps, as a way to hold the stick steady as you bring the tool to it. The "mule" is hybrid of the German and Swiss designs (so yes, it's a woodworking joke, hahaha!), a version developed by Drew Langsner and Tom Dohaney. And it's the version I like best. I've built and used several versions of different types of shaving horses over the years, and they each have their advantages and disadvantages for different types of work. If you are specifically making branch handles, this is my favorite. You can get the plans online by looking for Drew and Toms plans at various sites, or if you aren't terribly excited about building your own, I and other makers sell them online.

How it works.

Find a comfortable seat on the mule and place the stick into the jaws of the mule. You may have to adjust the ratcheting clamp on the vice to hold your stick. You should be able to turn it with ease, and clamp down by putting pressure on the pedal. Sometimes the stick will be pointing towards you, sometimes sliding past your body on a diagonal.

Now that you have this clamping business down, let's go for the drawknife.

DRAWKNIFE

A drawknife is a tool you hold with both hands that you pull or push to do the majority of the handle shaping. Think of it as one blade of a scissor. You generally pull it toward you, holding it on a slight diagonal as you go. You should hear a very even slicing sound, getting even pieces almost like peeling a potato, and have big smoothly cut pieces coming off of your work.

A nice start into the bark.

Note the clean facets the drawknife produces. If you are not getting this type of finish, it is time to review sharpening.

Reversing the direction to prevent tear out while approaching a switch in the grain.

CREATING A HANDLE (continued)

DIY BREAKOUT
Sharpening a Drawknife

The same basic sharpening principles apply. I originally started by putting a clamp on each side of the drawknife on the edge of the table, and bringing the stone to it at a consistent angle. The drawknife is a great tool to learn sharpening on. Generally speaking, the bevel of the blade is very large, and finding that angle can be easier than on a smaller tool.

Bring the stone to the tool, and work over the entire tool until you have a small burr running the entire length of the tool.

Flip over the tool and lap the back, until the burr has folded back to the other side. Move up the consecutive grits as before until you get through the extra fine (or 4000) grit. You could strop it as well if that's your thing.

I, nowadays, brace the tool against my body like this, bring the stone to the tool and sharpen as above.

If you're using a found drawknife, I encourage you to try using it bevel up and bevel down. Generally, one side will cut deeper, but really a lot of this is personal preference for the work you're doing.

If you are new to sharpening, cover the entire bevel with a permanent marker so you can see where you are landing with your stone. A good steady hand will slowly remove the marker like a growing pool from the high spots outward. You should not notice an irregular pattern caused by shifting your angle.

On some drawknives, but not all, the upper ridge can act as a guide to give you the correct angle to hold the stone at. Try to find a grip that allows you to hold the stone consistently as you move across the bevel.

Some drawknives I enjoy working with:
→ An 8" or 10" Dunlap.
→ A Greenlee.
→ Any one you can find.

The third one is especially true. A word of note: tool steel, or steel sharp enough to keep an edge while you use it, used to be quite expensive, so a lot of the older drawknives are made with laminated blades, a less expensive steel holding a small bar of tool steel. Often times you can actually see the lamination lines in an old tool. If the one you find is too skinny in the middle, or you can see there is no tool steel left, you may want to skip it for one that can hold an edge. A used drawknife in decent order will usually cost you $20-$50.

Let's try this!

Sit on your shaving mule with your stick in front of you, place both hands on the drawknife and pull towards you with the bevel facing up. Now flip the drawknife bevel side down and do the same. Always keep both hands on the tool when in use. You will find different drawknives work differently one way or the other, often cutting deeper with it bevel up. Play around with this until you decide which combination you like with the drawknife you have. The blade should easily slice through the wood you are trying to shape.

When you approach a knot, approach it from both sides. This may mean rotating the stick in the vice, or pushing the drawknife away from you, a technique you will also often use. In general, you can think of it like one blade of a pair of scissors, approaching at a diagonal, and listen for a smooth cutting sound. If you're moving through a knot or dense spot, try taking smaller bites. Think of it as removing a mountain: take a little off the top, don't attack it from the base and expect the whole thing to move.

After your stick is completely cleaned with a drawknife, continue using the shaving mule as a clamp and switch over to the spokeshave.

SPOKESHAVE

A spokeshave is like a mini drawknife where the depth of the blade is already set.

Some spokeshaves I like are:
→ Lie Nielsen Boggs Spokeshave
→ Any spokeshave you can find.

A good used spokeshave should run you around $40-$50.

Spokeshave and drawknife, the perfect combo!

CREATING A HANDLE (continued)

DIY BREAKOUT
Sharpening a Spokeshave

To sharpen a spokeshave, start by removing the blade from the tool body. Place the stone on a bench. If you find it slides around in the sharpening process, you may need to clamp it down, or add a non-slip mat to help it stay in place. Now bring the blade to the stone. Hold the blade at an angle so the bevel will meet the stone completely.

Brace your fingers so that the angle is easy to keep with your body. There is a bit of an audible click, like a latch fully closing when you have it held at the proper angle. Peek from the side to make sure there is no light shining between the tool and the stone.

Move the blade side to side like you are a robot, not letting your position stray from holding the blade evenly. Slow and steady is great if you're new to this, occasionally checking your blade to see if, yes, same as before, you have a burr over the entire edge. The permanent marker technique is recommended here as well if you are newer to sharpening.

Continue to sharpen through all of the stone grits as before, doing one side, then a few passes on the opposite side to remove the burr. Continue until the blade is sharp.

To put the blade back, place the body of the tool on a flat surface and gently place the blade back in the body of the tool. Tighten down any screws to hold the blade in place. This will generally give you the correct working depth for the tool. Test the blade depth: It should be easy to use, and you should get thin, even shavings from the tool.

If you are new to sharpening, cover the entire bevel of the blade with permanent marker. This will help you see if you are sharpening evenly and consistently.

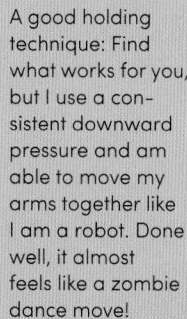

A good holding technique: Find what works for you, but I use a consistent downward pressure and am able to move my arms together like I am a robot. Done well, it almost feels like a zombie dance move!

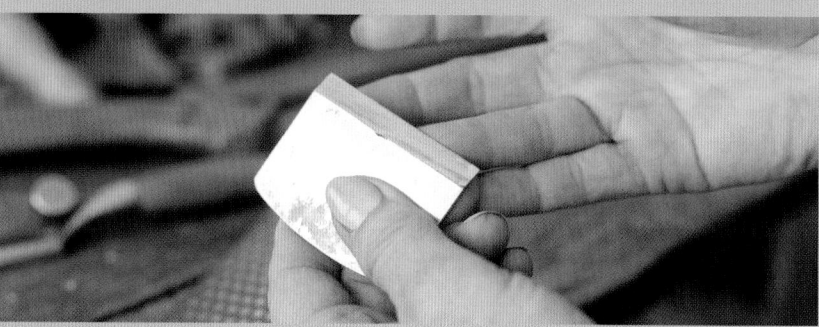

You use the spokeshave by holding it in both hands, and pulling or pushing it in the direction of the grain. This should give you small, even facets, forming a rounded, but nicely faceted surface, which for me is the end goal.

Finish up

Spokeshave the stick until it is generally complete. At this point it should be pretty close to complete, excepting a few touch-ups we will get to with a knife.

You're close. You can call it good. Or you can use that sharp knife of yours and clean up those little spots around the knots always making small cuts in the direction of the grain to prevent tear out. You can also use the knife to bevel, or round the top of your broomstick. For more information on knives, see pages 13-15.

POLISSEUR

I have Emmet Van Driesche to thank for introducing me to the polisher, or *polisseur*, a 14th century French tool for burnishing. The one I use is essentially a pot scrubber tied on both sides. The goal is to crush wood fibers slightly into a smooth finish. You can get a nearly glass-like finish this way.

To finish handles, I don't use sandpaper (except for on stringy grain). I don't love sanding, and I love the natural finish the *polisseur* offers. No sanding leaves all the slight facets of the handwork, but a very smooth-to-the-touch finish.

You did it! Stick complete! Now let's tie a cobwebber on one of these, shall we?

Using the spokeshave.

Reversing for a knot.

A well used (over 5 years!) and a new polisseur made of broomcorn. Making your own is a great little broom-making exercise. The ends are great for polishing spoon bowls!

Using the middle of the *polisseur* for crushing the wood fibers smooth.

Floor Brooms
COBWEBBERS

Have corner cobwebs on your ceiling? Let's fix it with a cobwebber broom! Making a cobwebber is a great place to start if you have never made a broom with a handle. It weaves in two layers (or one if you chose to!) and teaches the fundamental movements needed to make a broom with a handle. This will also use the techniques for weaving a woven handle from the hand brooms section, so feeling proficient there will make bigger brooms much easier to make.

TOOLS & MATERIALS
- five gallon bucket, ¾ full with warm water
- craft broomcorn: 20 nice stalks and 15 whatever stalks (see description)
- drill with an ⅛" drill bit
- cobwebber stick
- floor spool or foot brake
- nylon for weaving
- knife
- scissors
- jerk string

THE SETUP

A cobwebber broom is a long, tall, skinny sweep, long enough to reach the corners of your ceiling. Tall ceilings? Make a tall cobwebber! I like to use an extra long and lightweight stick for these so I can really reach for the nooks and crannies! I am telling you, this tool is a home-cleaning game-changer.

1 This first step is done several hours in advance of actually sitting down to weave, so plan accordingly. From your selection of 22" (or so!) hurl, select 20 with really nice stalks. A nice stalk is something you weave with that is seen. This is your outer decorative layer. I look for thin stalks that are about a pencil-width in thickness with no cracks or splits and are fairly long. Then I look for 15 with stalks that can be cracked or short. Depending on your batch of broomcorn, you may have very little that qualifies for one batch or the other, but do your best to sort them out.

2 Use a rubber band or string around the middle of each bundle, leaving yourself enough room for the stalks at the bottom to be able to freely soak up the water. Leave this to soak, and we will weave in a few hours.

FLOOR BROOMS: *COBWEBBERS*

3   Go ahead and set up similarly to hand brooms. Wind your string around the center of your spool, have your jerk string nearby, and your soaked bucket of broomcorn.

4   Drill a small hole big enough for your string to pass through. I use a ⅛" drill bit in a drill (see photo). Drill a small hole about 2" up from the end of the broom.

5   Take the end of your string from the floor spool and slide it through the hole. Tie it tightly to itself using a square knot. (Note, if you want to add a brad or staple at this point for extra security you can.)

6   Pull your bundle of less good looking stalks from the water and have it nearby. Also place your good looking bundle within reach (and unbundle it, but don't mix the two!). We will start with the less good looking bundle.

Author's note: Some of the stalks in these photos have been slimmed down: We will cover the process for this in the next chapter. Don't worry about this step for now; weave on!

THE HANDMADE BROOM

LET'S WEAVE

From now on through the entire weaving process, you will be pulling HARD on the line. There are little moments where you let the slack go intentionally, but generally you are pulling tension the whole time. You should be able to play that nylon twine like a washtub bass. That's how much tension you have!

7 Hold the stick with the long side headed out past your dominant hand, and put tension on the line.

8 Slide your first stalk from your not-as-good pile up and under the line, creasing it at ¼" above the knuckle. After you add it, make a small pulling-up motion (toward your face), to really secure it in place. Slide the next stalk beside the one you just added in the same manner. You may find you need to do a slight unwinding by rolling your wrists forward like you are going over the "handlebars" of your broom to get the next stalk snugly beside the one you just added. Keep adding stalks until you have added all the way around the handle.

9 Make a tight band wrapping three times around.

88   THE HANDMADE BROOM

FLOOR BROOMS: *COBWEBBERS*

10   Spiral up about 1" on a diagonal. Do not go too high on this, as you will have to do a decorative weave to cover this entire layer.

11   Make another band wrapping three times. Always wrapping towards the top of the stick.

12   Spiral back down to where you started and make another band directly on top of the first band you made. This doesn't have to be neat, just secure!

13   Keeping tension on the line as you do so, cut off your stalks at a steep angle ¼" above the top band.

> **NOTE:** *things to look for as we go*
>
> You want to add this next layer DIRECTLY on top of where the last one started, meaning your band over this layer sits on top of the band below. Sounds easy enough, but the tendency will be for this layer to ride up above, so make sure your string is tracking as you wrap to be directly on top of the layer below. A good example of proper tracking can be seen in photo 15.

THE HANDMADE BROOM

LET'S WEAVE (continued)

14 Now we will add the top layer. This step uses the same techniques as weaving a decorative top on a hand broom, so if you remember the steps, go for it, or here's a review:

15 Add the nicer looking bundle one stalk at a time, staying careful to be directly on top of where you added the last layer. Note, this may take some swinging of the handle to keep the tracking right for the entire layer.

16 Make a tight band of three, remember to breathe, and let's weave!

17 Tie the top fluffy end of your broom loosely with a cord, rubber band, or piece of leather so you can weave without worry of breaking off the stalks.

18 Using your thumb at the base of the stalk, gently lift a stalk SIDEWAYS, as you did with the woven top sweeper at the same time you swoop the broom, this allows the line to easily pass underneath. Each time you pass a stalk, there is a slight tug you do to nestle the string as close to the last row as possible. The whole motion is a flip, a swoop of the brush, and a cinching down.

90   THE HANDMADE BROOM

FLOOR BROOMS: *COBWEBBERS*

19 The string will go where it wants to if you don't take a moment to tell it where to go with a light cinching motion. Always tighten the string down where YOU want it to go. Sometimes this will involve wiggling the stalk like a loose tooth to make sure the string slides all the way up to where you want it to be.

20 Head over the next stalk, under the following, until you have gone all the way around.

21 For an over under pattern, or plain weave, you should be going over the one you went previously under to make a pattern of squares. If you are going over the same one you went over before, go back and split a fatter stalk in half. You could count ahead of time to come up with an odd number of plants, but I like to let the full amount fit as they should and split a stalk if I need to to make it work out. I use my thumbnail to run down the reed, but a small knife works as well (pictured). Continue with each row, always using that same sequence of lift, swoop, cinch until you have at least woven it taller than the layer underneath.

22 You can weave as high as you like, but at some point the stalks will start to get brittle, and you will find they want to break. During one of your weaving sessions, I encourage you to find this edge.

THE HANDMADE BROOM

LET'S WEAVE (continued)

23 When you reach the top, make another band of at least three wraps pulling TIGHT, adding your jerk string in heads up in the direction you are going as you complete the first rotation of the band.

24 Bracing your winding as you did with your hand brooms, keep tension with your thumb behind the jerk string, and cut the line around 3" in front of the broom.

25 Quickly slide your end through the loop of your jerk string and pull it through, pulling hard on the tail.

26 Cut the tail of the cord to ¼" or so and using your awl, tuck it behind one of the woven squares.

27 Trim the top of your weave as desired. I like to trim it fairly even with a flat cut ¼" above the band.

28 Hang your broom to dry, bristles down where it can air out.

You did it! Your first woven top! If all your weaving was a disaster, as long as your bands are tight, the broom will hold. It will get better with time. Just nail the start and the landing for now and you will have a perfectly functional broom!

FLOOR BROOMS: *COBWEBBERS*

Let your cobwebber dry for a day or so, and when the inside layer close to the stick where you soaked it seems pretty dry, it is time to stitch it in the round. I like to sit on a tall stool to do this, as there is a lot of spinning of the broom. Sit on the stool, and hold your broom handle down, so your stitching is about at eye level.

WEAVING IN THE ROUND

29   Holding your broomcorn into a nice round flame shape, throw a rubber band, string, or tie around the broom (I use a strip of leather as I find it holds itself in that spot nicely.)

30   Get your stitching needles out (or your sawed-off hacksaw blades!). It's time to stitch.

31   Cut a piece of string from your spool that is two arm wingspans in length. (This will be more than plenty for the cobwebber. Take note of the excess and adjust accordingly next time.

THE HANDMADE BROOM   93

WEAVING IN THE ROUND *(continued)*

 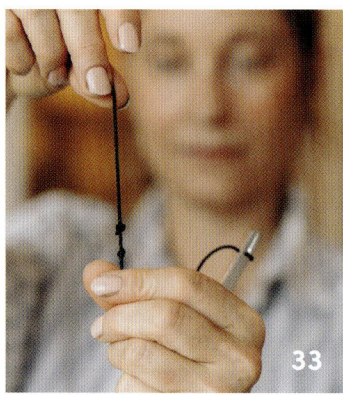

32 Secure the line to the needle. I tend to just use a criss cross, like beginning to tie my shoes, and am careful to not pull it off my needle, a square knot works just as well.

33 Tie two small knots at the end of the line.

34 Dive your needle through the center of your broom and pull the string almost entirely through until your knots are buried in the center of your broom.

35 At this point, put your needle down nearby, and gently, holding the line near the broom, rotate the broom twice spiraling the string around the broom as you go towards the fluffy end of the broom.

FLOOR BROOMS: *COBWEBBERS*

36 When you have two neat bands around the broom, keeping tension, pick the needle back up and dive through the center of the broom, coming straight out the other side above the band. Here you make a stitch. Go below the band and straight through the broom, diving out the other side, coming out above the band.

37 Make another stitch here. If you think of what you have done so far as points on a compass, you've stitched North and South. Now you will head for East and West, changing directions with the needle inside the broom, and repeating the same stitching process. This will give you four stitches evenly spaced around the circle, pulling the thread through tightly each time.

THE HANDMADE BROOM   95

WEAVING IN THE ROUND (continued)

38 Now you will head across the broom but aim for splitting to the midpoints between each stitch: NE, NW, SE, SW. After you have come out of the broom for the start of your eighth and final stitch, but before you do the final half stitch, tie a small knot in the line, about ½" away from the broom.

39 Dive the needle in to complete the last stitch, burying the knot in the broom.

40 Cut the line and you've done it! You stitched the first band on your cobwebber.

FLOOR BROOMS: *COBWEBBERS*

41 Repeat the process about 2" up towards the sweeping end of the broom, or as many times as you would like, making a stitched band each time. One will work, more makes it fancy. You usually see two bands on a cobwebber.

42 You did it! Go move those cobwebs!

Now that you have a thoroughly clean ceiling, let's make some for the floors!

Floor Brooms

TRADITIONAL APPALACHIAN WITH BROOMCORN

TOOLS & MATERIALS
- five gallon bucket, ¾ full with warm water
- craft broomcorn: 25 nice stalks and 25 whatever stalks
- a drill with an ⅛" drill bit
- broom stick
- floor spool or foot brake
- nylon for weaving
- knife
- scissors
- jerk string

There are two general types of Appalachian floor sweeps: one tied with the full stalk attached to the hurl (called craft broomcorn), and one tied with just hurl. Both styles make a workhorse of a broom—built to last until the bristles wear down. If made correctly, they grab more dirt, and are far easier to use than a store-bought broom!

The difference in style is mostly preference, but also setup. Weaving with just the hurl is often easily and quickly achieved with a stand up kick winder, discussed in Tools for the Long Haul chapter. I personally love the stalk-on classic Appalachian sweeper. It is a joy to weave, and the first full sweep I learned, so we will start there in the big broom projects!

THE SETUP

Starting with craft broomcorn means we will be weaving the stalk of the actual plant. Weaving the stalks can take some practice. I introduce slimming down the stalks in this section, which can make them a bit more delicate. If you are having trouble with them cracking, I suggest going back to using the whole stalk, make sure you are gently supporting it at the base as you lift them, and go slowly the first time. Practice really clarifies how to snug the string, and where to pull and scoot for a nice, tight weave.

Start the process with sorting through the broomcorn to get what we need to make an excellent sweeper. Note: This part can be done far in advance of weaving, and the broomcorn will soak for several hours before we begin the weaving process.

1 To sort through your broomcorn, you are looking for plants with a length of hurl 16-18". Lay out a marker, a ruler works well, or a board cut to length with 2" increments on its face and sort your broomcorn by hurl length into different piles. A pile of 14", 16", 18", 20", 22" and really long are good increments to work with. For this loose sweep, we will use our 18" hurl length of plants. (Note: If you plan to flat cut your broom, you don't have to worry about that part as much.)

FLOOR BROOMS: *TRADITIONAL APPALACHIAN WITH BROOMCORN*

2 After you've sorted for length of hurl, sort through your pile of 18" ones to find 25 with good looking stalks attached. For me, that means approximately pencil-width (or smaller!), 6"–8" (or longer) and with no obvious cuts or blemishes in them. My nicer pile is at the bottom of the photo, to give you an idea.

3 Bundle this pile together, tying a string loosely about halfway up the bundle and submerge in a 5 gallon bucket with enough warm water to cover the entire knuckle of the plant.

4 Find 25 plants with whatever kind of stalks attached to the hurl—broken, no stalks, anything really that didn't fall into the first category.

5 Add those to the bucket in the same manner as the first bundle.

6 Let these soak for a few hours. This is when I get the stick ready, typically.

THE HANDMADE BROOM

LET'S WEAVE

This broom start is almost the same as a cobwebber, but has a second layer underneath, so really three layers in total. Try to keep your underneath layers to as few stalks as possible to span the distance, so really squish them flat, so each stalk takes up as much space as possible, and try to prevent them from bunching together as you add them!

7 Since the broom has so many layers (keep in mind it takes nearly 50 plants to make a full-sized sweeper!), I like to slim down my stalks by splitting them in half.

I do this by running a broad knife like a wedge up the back of the stalk. After I find the grain of the stalk, I let my knife run up the stalk just below the knuckle. It does take a little practice to not just chop off the stalk, so start with your inner layer.

You may notice how I support the start of my cut with a stack of my knuckles. This is what lets me find the correct angle into the broomcorn.

8 After you have all of the stalks you plan to use slimmed down, weave away if that's all the instruction you need, or follow along step by step for the rest!

Gather yourself, supplies, and string as before. You may want a towel or leather apron in your lap for this next part as the broomcorn will be wet.

FLOOR BROOMS: *TRADITIONAL APPALACHIAN WITH BROOMCORN*

9 Drill a small hole in the stick approximately 2" from the bottom. I choose which side to tie the broom heads on based on feel. I hold the stick as I will use it and feel which end makes sense to hold. The hole you drill should be just over the diameter of the string, so there isn't a lot of play in the string.

> **NOTE:** *no drill, no problem*
>
> Traditionally, a lot of brooms were also started by driving a nail or staple into the handle.
>
> Using a small tack hammer, drive an upholstery tack or small nail halfway into the broom handle. Loop your string around the tack and drive it firmly. Make sure your string is firmly attached before continuing.

10 Put the string through the hole and tie a small square knot, securing the line to itself. You can add a small tack or staple here for extra security.

THE HANDMADE BROOM

LET'S WEAVE (continued)

11 To review adding stalks: adding one at a time, always rotating the handle towards you, follow the same steps that you did for making a cobwebber. You will be pulling HARD on the line. There are little moments where you let the slack go intentionally, but generally you are pulling tension the whole time. You should be able to play that nylon twine like a washtub bass that's how much tension you have!

12 Slide your first stalk from your not-as-good pile up and under the line, creasing it at ¼" above the knuckle. After you add it, make a small pulling-up motion (toward your face), to really secure it in place. Slide the next stalk beside the one you just added in the same manner. You may find you need to do a slight unwinding by rolling your wrists forward like you are going over the "handlebars" of your broom to get the next stalk snugly beside the one you just added. Keep adding stalks until you have added all the way around the handle.

FLOOR BROOMS: *TRADITIONAL APPALACHIAN WITH BROOMCORN*

13 It is very easy to end up with too many stalks under the line by having them all bunch together as you loosen the tension slightly to add a new one. When I am adding these layers, I like to think of adding as few stalks as possible. If you end up with a giant wad of a broom on your first one, don't worry; I did too! It took me hours to weave, so do what you can to keep your broom down in size.

14 After you have added stalks all the way around, make a tight band, wrapping three times around.

15 Spiral up about 1" on a diagonal.

16 Make another band wrapping three times.

17 Spiral back down to where you started, and make another band directly on top of the first band you made.

THE HANDMADE BROOM   105

LET'S WEAVE *(continued)*

18 At this point you can choose to add a small tack or staple to the work for extra security if you want. Just drive it near your line and have the staple span the band or the tack head to secure it into place. You can add one to each of the under layers if you would like.

19 Keeping tension on the line as you do so, cut off your stalks at a steep angle ¼" above the top band. You may find yourself unraveling a pass as you do. It's all good! Just add it back when you are done.

20 Now we will add the middle layer, using the remaining stalks from your less-than-perfect pile.

21 Add the stalks one at a time as before until you have a middle layer that starts directly on top of the layer below it. It will take some intentional moving of the broom to get these layers to track right on top of each other.

22 Spiral up the broom handle until you are above the layer below, tight against the handle itself. Make a tight band of three that firmly affixes this layer to the handle.

106   THE HANDMADE BROOM

FLOOR BROOMS: *TRADITIONAL APPALACHIAN WITH BROOMCORN*

23 Spiral back down to the start, and make another band of three, overlapping where you just made the layer below.

24 Cut the top at an angle as before. You can also repeat this process exactly as written for your next or outer layer. If you realize weaving isn't your thing, you can still get a nice working broom without all the weaving involved, so choose your own adventure!

THE HANDMADE BROOM   107

OUTER LAYER

Now it's time for the outer layer. A lot of first-time weavers find themselves very hunched at this point. It is easy to overgrip, and follow the tension of the line almost all the way down to the floor! Try to remind yourself to sit up now and again, but also know ease will come with practice. This step uses the same techniques as weaving a decorative top on a hand broom, so if you remember the steps, go for it, or here's a review. Let's weave!

25 Get your bundle of 25 nicer looking stalks out. Add the nicer looking bundle one stalk at a time in the same manner as before until you have a full layer around the broom.

26 Add your stalks one at a time to the broom, gently snugging each stalk under the line about ¼" up from the knuckle of the plant. This layer also happens directly on top of the previous layers.

27 Keep adding in each stalk, rolling the broom slightly forward like you are turning handlebars to add a stalk, then rolling back and pulling the whole broom with both hands up toward your face in a quick, tightening motion. After you have added stalks all the way around the broom, make a tight band of three around the stalks. (Or more, this part will be seen, so it is a bit of an aesthetic decision, here.)

FLOOR BROOMS: *TRADITIONAL APPALACHIAN WITH BROOMCORN*

28 Now let's begin the decorative weave. Using your thumb at the base of the reed, gently lift a reed SIDEWAYS at the same time you swoop the broom. This allows the line to easily pass under the stalk. Each time you pass a reed, there is a slight tug you do to nestle the string as close to the last row as possible. The whole motion is a stalk flip, a swoop of the brush, and a cinching down.

29 The string will go where it wants to if you don't take a moment to tell it where to go with a light cinching motion. Always tighten the string down where YOU want it to go. Sometimes this will involve wiggling the stalk like a loose tooth to make sure the string slides all the way up to where you want it to be.

30 Route the string over the next stalk and under the following one. Repeat the pattern until you have gone all the way around.

31 Now you should be going over the one you previously went under to make a pattern of squares. If you are going over the same one you went over before, go back and split a fatter stalk in half lengthwise.

OUTER LAYER (continued)

32 Continue with each layer, always using that same sequence of lift, swoop, cinch, until you have at least made it taller than the layer underneath.

33 How high do you weave? You can weave as high as you would like. At some point the stalks will start to get brittle, and you will find they want to break. As long as your weaving is taller than the layers underneath, the stopping point is up to you.

34 When you reach the top, add your jerk string in heads up in the direction you are going, make another band of at least three, and pull TIGHT. Holding tension with your thumb, cut the line several inches beyond the jerk string, thread it through the "eye" of the jerk string, and pull hard on the tail in a quick motion. You did it! If all your weaving was a disaster, as long as your bands are tight, the broom will hold. It will get better with time. Just nail the start and the landing for now and you will have a perfectly functional broom.

FLOOR BROOMS: *TRADITIONAL APPALACHIAN WITH BROOMCORN*

35 Cut the tail of the string around ¼" long and using your awl, tuck it under one of the weaves.

36 Trim the top of your broom with a sharp knife.

37 Before we flat weave the broom or hang it to dry, I like to drill the handle in the correct direction. This will involve what is called balancing the broom. The broom will have a spot where it likes to roll to with gravity if you have chosen a woodland handle. You can balance it on your lap like I do in the photo, or hold your arms out in front of you, palms up, and put the broom across your arms. Let the broom roll until it balances. That is how the broom likes to sit, and you should drill your handle hole parallel to the floor, and later flat weave it parallel to this direction. This will prevent the broom from rolling in your hand as you sweep (trying to find its natural place of rest).

38 After finding the balance to it, drill a ¼" hole 1" down from the top of the broom using a portable drill. Thread your hang tie through the hole and tie it to itself with a square knot. Leave this to dry for a day or so. After the broom has dried it's time to flat weave it.

FLAT WEAVING

Flat weaving is what gives your broom its wide sweep. Especially with this style of large sweep, really take your time as you lay it in the clamp, making sure each side is laying well before you finally clamp it down. Your clamp will, to some degree, find a natural seating for the first row of stitching where it is above all the weaving and fastening happening on the inside of the broom.

NOTE: *a visual diagram*

As you flat weave, you will be making a pattern of Z's essentially in the broom where, if viewed from above, one stitch is opposite the previous one. For the next stitch, you travel within the broom to come out further down the broom, making a series of Z shapes that work as your stitching pattern. So let's get started!

39 Begin by laying your broom on the ground to get the clamp around it. Free the bolt and wing nut from one side of the clamp, and loosen the other side until it is wide enough to slide over the broom.

40 As you begin to get your broom sandwiched in the clamp, make sure the pieces of the broomcorn are sitting where you want them to go, especially as you tighten down the clamp. They can have a tendency to slide to the side of the broom due to pressure.

FLOOR BROOMS: *TRADITIONAL APPALACHIAN WITH BROOMCORN*

41 Take your time with this part. There's no going back if you have an annoying gap where you can see the layers underneath. This is where you will also really see it if your layers were not starting on top of each other. The layers below can show through.

42 Stand your broom upright on the ground. I usually like to sit on a taller stool or counter for this part. Spin your broom to check both sides one more time. Your pressure with the clamp should be quite tight.

43 Insert a small wire into the center of each side of the broom. This should be approximately 1½" below the clamp, which will keep the string from sliding down the V shape of the broom as you work.

44 Measure off two full arm lengths of string and attach them to your stitching needle. I use just an over-under, like the start of tying your shoes, but any knot you can undo quickly is fine.

45 Tie two small knots at the end of your string opposite of the needle.

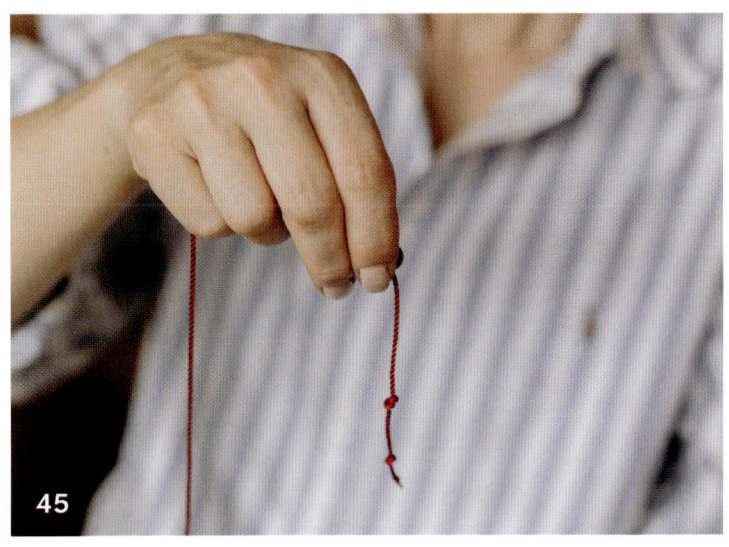

THE HANDMADE BROOM

FLAT WEAVING (continued)

46a

46b

47

46 Beginning with one side of the broom facing you, insert your needle about an inch back from the side. Weave your needle through the inside of the broom to come out the middle of the side between your wires and the clamp. Pull the string through the broom until your two knots are buried and all the rest of your string is pulled through. This part is really to anchor your flat weaving by burying the two knots.

47 At this point, I like to put down the needle in my lap and gently spin the broom twice around, stacking the string on top of itself up toward the clamp as I go.

FLOOR BROOMS: *TRADITIONAL APPALACHIAN WITH BROOMCORN*

48   This should make a small band going around the broom twice. After you are back at the staring point, maintain tension on the wraps you made by anchoring them with your hand. Then pick the needle up and slide it into the middle of the broom's side above the two rows, coming out about an inch into one of the sides of the broom above the two rows. On this first stitch, it's very important to pull gently. If you pull too hard, it can slide the whole thing down the V shape of your broom.

49   Now take your needle and directly below where you came out, dive into the broom, coming out above the band on the opposite side. This should make one stitch over the band you created.

50   Rotate the broom so you have flipped it 180 degrees so you can see where your needle has come out. Make your second stitch, again starting above and exiting below the band. This time, rather than coming out directly across, travel within the broom to come out an inch down the broom from where you started.

THE HANDMADE BROOM   115

FLAT WEAVING (continued)

51a

51b

51 Repeat the process of making a small stitch, making a stitch opposite it, and then traveling within the broom to start the sequence again. Repeat all the way down the broom, until you have evenly spaced stitches.

> **NOTE:** *style choices:*
>
> Not every broom maker stitches the same way. Some go one way and call it good, some stitch down and back, and some make small X shapes on the ends by making their stitches tiny diagonals. (Darold, who I learned from, called it pickup three. He would count over three individual straws, and make his stitches small diagonals, and make little X shapes on the ends to tie off his work.) After you get the basics of stitching, it's a choose-your-own-adventure of styles!

FLOOR BROOMS: *TRADITIONAL APPALACHIAN WITH BROOMCORN*

52 I then make a small stitch on the very side of my broom, pull my small wires out from the sides, and head back towards the starting point, splitting each gap in half with another stitch.

53 After stitching all the way back to the beginning, start the final stitch on the side of the broom. After exiting the broom to start the stitch, tie two small knots in the line about an inch away from the broom itself. Then dive in to complete the stitch, but this time drag your needle several inches into the broom to bury the knot.

54 Cut the line where it comes out. This is going to secure your stitching to the broom. That's all that holds it? Yup! That's it.

THE HANDMADE BROOM   117

FLAT WEAVING (continued)

55a

55b

56

55 Slide the clamp towards the sweeping end of the broom and tighten it down. Reinsert the small wires about 1½" down and attach your two arm's length of string to the needle as before. Repeat the process from beginning to end to stitch this next row. And another and another. Really, it is up to you how many rows you stitch; each row makes the broom stiffer. I like to stitch two rows, then sweep with it to decide if I want to add another.

56 Gently trim off the stray or extra long pieces in your broom.

> **NOTE:** *shoulders and sides*
> You will notice that brooms have, well, a broom shape. This is often caused by adding either what is called shoulders or sides to your broom. You get shoulders by adding an extra bundle of broomcorn to the side of your broom in the broom-making process, usually underneath on the first layer, very much like a Hawks Tail. Shoulders are like sides, except as you add the broomcorn to create sides, you add it facing upwards and then fold it downwards to make an even more besom-y looking broom! In the project with loose hurl, we will add sides to the broom, and you can add shoulders if you'd like. This is a process you can do in either style of large sweep.

FLOOR BROOMS: *TRADITIONAL APPALACHIAN WITH BROOMCORN*

57 Try it out! Sweep the floor! This should feel like a fairly gentle and ergonomically friendly process, and should work much better than a store-bought broom. If it feels awkward, see if you can troubleshoot: Did you balance your stick properly? Do the proportions feel correct? Make adjustments with each new broom, learning as you go.

57

FINE TUNING

The variations on this one are pretty much endless: What type of stick you use, the weaving pattern, but here are some things to troubleshoot:

→ Are your layers directly on top of each other? Can you see a little spiraling section where your string starts into your bands (a telltale sign)? If so, work to really track your string so each layer is directly on top of the previous. Making the string line up sometimes involves holding your broom at odd angles, so don't be afraid to do so.

→ Is your flat weaving tight and even? I think a little variation is cute, but you want to be making that choice. Are you accidentally making tiny diagonal stitches? Notice the pattern, and adjust accordingly.

→ Is your flat weave bunching a bit? You might be pulling too tightly on your first few stitches. Sometimes this can happen from tightening your bands too much on your first few stitches, causing an odd bunching. It also can happen if your clamp needs to be set wider for the top row (my clamp is usually set to the middle hole for my first row, the outer hole for the last row).

THE HANDMADE BROOM

Floor Brooms

TRADITIONAL APPALACHIAN WITH JUST THE HURL

Brooms made with hurl more closely resemble the hardware store sweeps, but tie them on a unique handle with a nice decorative weave on top, and you have a beautifully balanced one-of-a-kind creation. You can still make a "loose end" sweep with just the hurl—it is a matter of using different lengths on the layers. So let's make one!

TOOLS & MATERIALS

- five gallon bucket, ¾ full with warm water
- large handful (12 oz. or so each) of 16", 18", and 20" hurl. Note, if you only have 18" hurl, slide the first group up as if it is 16" and that will let you approximate a loose sweep in a hurl broom.
- drill with an ⅛" drill bit
- broom stick
- floor spool or foot brake
- nylon for weaving
- knife
- scissors
- jerk string

THE SETUP

Let's make a full size sweep with just the hurl. Spacing the hurl around the broom takes a bit of practice to do evenly and smoothly. Broom makers with a lot of practice will look like they are almost throwing all the hurl on at once in a smooth motion. Give yourself time, pay attention to the spacing, and enjoy the process.

1 For this broom, we will use different lengths of hurl so we can maintain having a loose sweep. If you planned to flat cut your broom at the end of this project, you can use all the same size of hurl.

2 I like to use 16" for the inner layer, 18" for the middle layer, and 20" for the outer layer. Each layer will require a large handful of the broomcorn hurl (approximately 12 oz., depending on the diameter of the handle). For this first one, grab a little more than you think you need. The different sizes allow you to still have a loose sweep feel with your final broom.

3 You will also need a bucket with about 5" of warm water in the bottom of it, big enough to soak the ends of the broomcorn you will attach to the handle.

FLOOR BROOMS: *TRADITIONAL APPALACHIAN WITH JUST THE HURL*

4 Begin by drilling a small ⅛" hole into your broomstick, about 2" up from the end of the broomstick. Thread your string through the hole, and tie it to itself using a small square knot, as you did with the previous project.

5 Place the 16" hurl in the bucket of water and hold it there for a long count of 5. You may want a towel or a leather apron in your lap to avoid soaking your pants on this one.

6 The process for adding the hurl is very similar to how you added the craft broomcorn in the last full-sized sweep. This time, though, you will add loose pieces in small bundles. Go ahead and divide your 16" hurl into 4 or 5 bunches, as seen in the photos.

THE HANDMADE BROOM 123

LET'S WEAVE

In step 8 we will be adding sides to the broom. This is the spot where you can also add shoulders, or shoulders and sides, if you so choose. All the options will affect how wide and boxy your broom shape is. I recommend playing with all the sizes of both until you settle on a combo you like, or have a handle on a repertoire you can choose from on a given occasion.

7 Add the 16" hurl around the handle, tightening it down with the string as you go. I like to split the total amount into bundles as if I am making a Turkey Wing. Divide it into 4-6 bundles you can add as you go. After you have added the bundles evenly around the stick, make a tight band around the hurl, going around the broom three times. This band should be so tight it squeezes the broomcorn like a belt. Now we will add sides.

8 Much like a Hawks Tail, add an extra bundle of broomcorn to each side of the broom. Start with a bundle about 2 oz, or a solid handful. You can always make these bigger or smaller on the next one. This will add small sides to your broom. This is also where you can add shoulders if you would like!

FLOOR BROOMS: *TRADITIONAL APPALACHIAN WITH JUST THE HURL*

9 Wrap around the entire thing three more times, then cut off the broomcorn ¼" above the band at a steep angle. This will give you a nice angle so your next layer can sit snugly close to this one. Drive a staple or nail in at this point if you choose for extra security.

10 Spiral up and onto the handle of your broom. The next layer for this style sits tightly above the one below it. Soak the 18" hurl for a count of 5, then add the 18" broomcorn in the same manner, lining up the fluffy ends of the broomcorn. After you've added it evenly around the broom, make a tight band of three over this layer.

11 Spiral up the broom 2" while rotating the broom, then make another tight band of three wraps. Now spiral back down to your starting place, and make another tight band directly on top of the first. Your next layer will sit directly on top of this layer.

12 Cut this layer like the last one.

THE HANDMADE BROOM

LET'S WEAVE (continued)

13 Now add the final 20" layer directly on top of the last one. This one is slightly different. For the final layer we will be sneaking our "spiraling up" behind the broomcorn in order to make it appear you have made two distinct bands. This way, if you decide not to add a woven top, you have a nice, clean top.

14 Soak the 20" hurl for a count of 5. Add it evenly around the broom and make a tight band of three. As you begin to sneak upward for your spiral, sneak the nylon behind the newly added broomcorn, then pop back on top when it is time to add your final band.

15 As you complete the first rotation of the band, add your jerk string in with the "eye" closer to the handle side of the broom.

FLOOR BROOMS: *TRADITIONAL APPALACHIAN WITH JUST THE HURL*

16 Make a tight band of three, then use your jerk string to complete your broom.

17 Tuck your tail in with an awl, and trim the top.

18 It's now time to hang the broom to dry for a day or so. Balance the handle as you did in the other full sweep you made: hold out your arms, palm up in front of you and place the broom on top of your arms. Allow the handle to naturally find its resting point on your outstretched arms. Drill the handle parallel to the ground and hang your broom to dry. Can you roll right into the woven top? You can! But a little extra dry time never hurt a broom.

THE HANDMADE BROOM

LET'S WEAVE (continued)

19 Begin by preparing the stalks as you did for a woven top sweeper. This prep should be completed several hours in advance. Begin by soaking a generous amount of stalks, 30 or so. Skipping any with obvious blemishes or defects, soak the stalks in warm water for a few hours or until they are pliable. Now follow the instructions on page 60 in the woven top sweeper section for preparing the stalks. The thinner you make them, the more weaving you will have to do, so when you are first learning to do so, try to find a balance between tiny and wide. A good ¼" wide is a nice starting place.

20 After your stalks are ready, have them at hand nearby, and let's weave!

21 Begin by wrapping your thread around the broom where the bottom band of your weaving starts. After you have gone around a full rotation, crisscross the line over itself and wrap a few more times.

22 At this point, you should be able to add tension into your pulling. Circle the band a final time, pulling tight. Then begin to add your stalks.

128   THE HANDMADE BROOM

FLOOR BROOMS: *TRADITIONAL APPALACHIAN WITH JUST THE HURL*

23   I like to crease my stalks with a little bend before adding them, but you can pre-crease all of them, marking what will go under the twine. Get rid of any stalks that crack at all. There is a good chance these will continue to crack as you go if you dont ditch them now!

24   Begin to add your stalks under the line, with the long part hanging down over the fluffy side of the broom.

25   Keep adding stalks as you continue your way around the broom. You want them snugly next to each other, not overlapping, but right next to each other. During the adding, you also want to make sure your thread is tracking just below where the band underneath is. This will keep these threads from showing when you fold them upward.

26   When you have added all the way around, go an extra time or two around to make sure your stalks are held down nicely.

THE HANDMADE BROOM   129

LET'S WEAVE (continued)

27 Spiral up about ¼", and go around the broom once so your line is tracking in a clean band.

28 Now comes the fun part. Gently slide your non-dominant hand under about a quarter of the stalks and gently fold them up. Continue folding them upwards in segments until you have all of the stalks ready to weave.

FLOOR BROOMS: *TRADITIONAL APPALACHIAN WITH JUST THE HURL*

29 Make a nice band of four wraps around your broom, establishing a starting point. Now we are ready to begin weaving.

> **NOTE:** *start small*
>
> I highly recommend using woven top hand brooms as an opportunity to get comfortable with weaving tops. It will give you a chance to learn the technique, figuring out how to not have split stalks (usually a matter of being gentle and supporting the stalk at the base, if it isn't just a difficult stalk). It will also give you a chance to try out different patterns in a less intense way. You may find when translating the technique to big brooms you have to maneuver the handle quite a bit to get the results you want, so practicing smaller goes a long way to letting you focus on that aspect when you step up to full sweeps.

30 Now we weave. Flip your starting stalk gently SIDEWAYS, supporting it at the base, and swoop your line underneath it, then cinch it down with a slight tug upward.

31 Rotate your broom slightly, keeping your string very close to your starting band. This is a matter of swinging the whole broom so you can track the string where you want it to go.

THE HANDMADE BROOM

LET'S WEAVE (continued)

32 Keep weaving under one stalk and over the next. Now we repeat the actions: Supporting the stalk at the base, swoop the line underneath, and rotate the broom so the line travels over the next stalk. Repeat this pattern all the way around your broom.

33 As you arrive back at the beginning of your weaving, you should be going over one stalk you went under before. If you are not, go back and split a slightly fatter stalk to make the count work out. There are lots of ways to arrive at having an odd number of stalks for a plain weave. This is how I do it.

34 Continue the pattern all the way up until you are past the layers underneath.

> **NOTE:** *many ways*
> Some broom makers will additionally taper the stalks as they go. There are times when I find this technique appropriate, such as scaling down the stalks to a tapering shape, and times that I don't. This first woven top does not, but feel free to try it on your future brooms.

FLOOR BROOMS: *TRADITIONAL APPALACHIAN WITH JUST THE HURL*

35 When you are back at the beginning, make a tight band. (I like to line up all my "entrances and exits," so to speak.) Add your jerk string in as you complete the first rotation. Then go over it 4–5 more times. Anchor the tension with your thumb, pull tight one last time, and snip the line in front of the jerk string.

36 Thread the jerk string and pull the tail.

37 Thats it! Find your place for the handle and allow this broom to dry before you go back and flat weave it.

Wow. The possibilities here are nearly infinite. Between stick selection and weaving patterns, this broom is a great place to play!

→ Troubleshooting: If you had trouble with your stalks cracking, even after you soaked them for a long time and sorted out the "crackers," make sure you are being gentle with them. Support them at the base, and scoot them to the side sneaking the line behind the stalk. Really, practice is where it is at for consistent, nice weaving.

→ Try variations in patterns and colors. Look to basket weavers for inspiration and try patterns out!

→ Play with the width, spacing, and colors on your flat weaving. So many options! I'm excited to see all the variations out there.

FINE TUNING

THE HANDMADE BROOM   133

Floor Brooms

HEARTH SWEEPS

TOOLS & MATERIALS

→ five gallon bucket, 5" full with warm water

→ 12 oz. of hurl. I use 18" in the photos.

→ a drill with an ⅛" drill bit

→ broom stick

→ floor spool or foot brake

→ nylon for weaving

→ knife and/or scissors

→ jerk string

→ axe and chopping block (a good knife can do this step more slowly)

→ wooden mallet or small sledge

→ small upholstery or other tacks. I like a 15 ga ¾" with a good head on the end

Hearth sweeps to me mean all the small versions of what we have made, plus a few clever variations. I put kids brooms and anything I design for the hearth in this category. If I am simply making a smaller version of one of the previous brooms, I skip a layer underneath, like I am making a cobwebber, then flat weave it! Voila, instant hearth broom. That is a great option, but there is another fun version of the hearth broom we will learn in this chapter.

THE SETUP

This broom I learned from fellow broom maker Hunter Elliott. It is essentially a Turkey Wing on a stick. I have seen lots of versions of how to make these. For this one, you will need to sharpen the point of a handle, and pound that in with a mallet to a started Turkey Wing. I sharpen this point with an axe on a chopping block, but a knife, or drawknife and shaving mule work wonders as well.

1 Pictured are a mallet for pounding the handle in (I like a good wooden mallet), a small hammer and tacks for fastening, and an axe for shaping the end of the handle.

2 Using the axe techniques you learned in the handle section, begin about 2" back from the end, and neatly taper one side of the handle then the opposite side. Then turn the handle to taper the remaining faces. You should have a neat, sharp pyramid to drive into the broom. Feel free to clean this up with a drawknife or knife if needed, but really, sharp and pointy works.

FLOOR BROOMS: *HEARTH SWEEPS*

3   Begin by making a Turkey Wing handbroom (see page 25). When you have 2 bundles left to add, pound that pointed handle into the Turkey Wing with a mallet. Add a tack for extra security.

4   Add the last two segments with the handle in place.

5   Add a tack at the end, by starting to drive a tack in, looping the line around the tack, then fully driving it in.

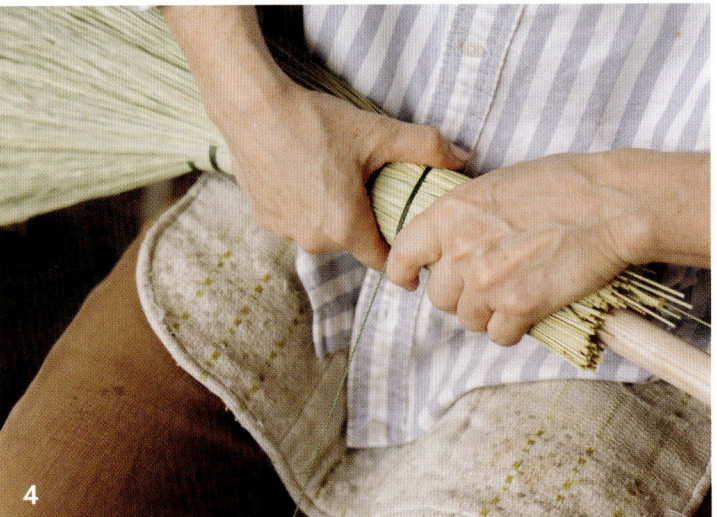

THE HANDMADE BROOM

THE SETUP (continued)

6 Trim above the line as if you are tapering while making hurl sweeps.

7 Continue to spiral the string up until it is on the handle section of your broom. Neatly adding the jerk string after you begin a final band on the handle of the broom.

8 Pull the jerk string through quickly and firmly as with previous brooms. You can neatly cut or trim the line at this point, but I recommend weaving a top over the whole lot of it. Here's where you can use your skills to weave a top either like a woven top sweeper (bottom up) or a handbroom (top down). Try different patterns and variations to see what you like best!

FLOOR BROOMS: *HEARTH SWEEPS*

9   Fan out your broom by hand before cutting the ends. This part always amazes me. You really can get quite a wide shape in the broom by forcing it that will stay in the final product.

10   We did it! We're done! We covered the basics (and a few not so basics!). That's gives you the foundation for Appalachian style broom making.

THE HANDMADE BROOM

Part 4
GOING DEEPER IN THE CRAFT

START EXPLORING

The first part of the book really gives you the fundamentals—the traditional jumping off point to understand the basics.

This next part gets more to the heart of some of the things I've been exploring within broom craft over the last decade. Partly driven from time in previous crafts, and partly from an obsession with natural and sustainable materials, this is just one direction the craft can open onto. It is exciting to think that after learning the basics, you can find your own way to obsess. Whether it's over native or natural fibers, traditional techniques from around the world, a mashup of crafts, you name it. Hopefully some of these will give you a basis to start your own exploring!

GOING DEEPER IN THE CRAFT

DIY BREAKOUT
Basing off of the work of others

It is an interesting thing these days: At the tap of a button, the internet can show you work from around the world to use as inspiration or a starting point. When I wanted to try alternative fibers, I saw a lot of wooden brush makers using Tampico fibers. I had never seen anyone weave hand brooms with it, but I was in a strong non-glue phase, so I called around to see if I could find longer Tampico to use. It is a blast to weave and led to a lot of exploration in hand brooms (traditionally used in rope making, and as a small pot scrubber in Northern Mexico). These days it's more widely played with in broom making, and more widely available, as are many other fibers as more and more folks explore alternatives to broomcorn.

This is how I like to use source ideas: Borrow a color palette here, try a different technique there. This is something that almost every modern maker has to think about: How do I relate the images I see online to my own work?

I personally like the stance that I gathered from the book Steal Like an Artist, by Austin Kleon and my version goes a bit like this:

1. If it's for your own home use, or for learning a technique that is beyond the traditional, copy away! It's how you learn and can move you forward in the craft.
2. If you are selling on a small, local scale, credit the original maker, better yet, reach out to them, and see if you can gain a better understanding of the lineage of the design. Have a conversation with them about the work.
3. If you are a large maker, or have a large platform, checking in with those conversations in step 2 can prevent any accidental "borrowing," and allow people to feel inspired by the sharing. And yes, if you are a large house, that might mean financially compensating a maker for their work.

That's my ideal. I also know, if you make something really rad, folks are going to want to replicate it. It is just part of making rad things and exploring new ideas. As much as possible, embrace your role as a trailblazer, celebrating the fact that you've moved the craft forward as a whole.

EXPLORING FIBERS

Looking at traditional brush fibers from around the world yields a ton of possibilities.

I highly recommend giving it a go with different material, such as Tampico, Arenga, Palm, Grass seed heads, and more local to where I live in Kentucky, broom sedge, and other grasses. Use the same techniques you already learned, then give it a go with weaving! Some of the results are quite pleasing. It's really a matter of going outside and collecting, or sourcing, and trying!

Experimenting with new fibers means making some odd ideas in the process! Different string weights will work with different fibers. Here are some of my early experiments with Tampico fiber: It's clear I was definitely exploring!

GOING DEEPER IN THE CRAFT

USING NATURAL ALTERNATIVES FOR BINDING

Natural Fibers for binding has been a deep rabbit hole for me. If you find images of Shaker brooms in this country, you can see metal, or a heavy 2mm 100lb test hemp twine in use.

I've made lots of mistakes in the name of exploration in this category, so here are some general things I've learned along the way to get you started.

Start with the above fibers. Try anything in the 2mm range to get a feel for the differences. One of the hard things with weaving natural fibers is that every batch is different. You may find success with one manufacturer, only to find it not able to hold up with the "same" fiber from a different manufacturer.

Do not use water in your hand brooms other than for decorative weaving if you choose to bind them with natural fibers. I learned the hard way that fibers stretch after you wet them, meaning you can make a perfectly lovely broom, and 2 weeks later you will find it has gone loose on you.

I personally don't weave with 1mm fiber anymore. I found for me, it does stretch over time, and does not make a broom that lasts very long. I wove quite a few hand brooms with a 1mm hemp, and while those photos still float around on the internet, I really dont recommend it.

In the name of exploration these days, I try and use something I am excited about around the studio for several months as a studio broom, or give it to someone

A closeup of a full sweep woven with 2MM hemp.

who will use it hard and report back. I am always testing new fibers, that's how I arrive at what I use. I keep testing as I go, and replace it if I find one I like better! That way, I can avoid the pain of telling supportive broom users that the fiber was maybe not the longest lasting option.

You can weave big brooms with natural fibers smaller than 2mm, it just takes practice!

I thought it was not possible when I first started. I was constantly breaking the line. I have found, with practice, that you pull TO THE BREAKING POINT and you can get enough tension out of it. Honestly, you can weave with nearly any diameter of nearly any fiber, it is really a question of will it stretch after the fact. It's a good idea to look at traditional constructions if you can! Take apart older brooms made from natural fibers, or head to a Shaker museum or craft collection. There is a lot to be learned from these brooms!

THE HANDMADE BROOM

DYEING BROOMCORN

Dyeing broomcorn is often a matter of finding a big enough vat (or bathtub) to fit it all in! I personally use a used deep turkey fryer setup for dyeing hurl, or long stainless steel sinks or tubs for longer broomcorn I can pour the whole mixture into. I hope to weld myself some longer pans as well for longer pieces.

Broomcorn is what is called in the dyeing world a closed cell fiber. Like cotton or other vegetal, it doesn't as readily take dye as wools and open cell fibers.

Brooms drying on a homemade drying rack after being rinsed clean. Please note: This process is hugely messy. Doing it outside or having a corner you know will end up covered in colors is highly recommended.

GOING DEEPER IN THE CRAFT

What this means is, as you are looking for recipes for dyeing, look for cotton, or other closed cell recipes, and follow the instructions from there. I personally love dyeing with natural dyes. A few tips to help you with your dyeing process:

→ Make sure you follow the entire recipe. If it says to mordant or scour, do so in the manner suggested.

→ When in doubt, add more heat and more time. I often leave things to take in color for a day or so, and make sure the bath is quite hot to start.

→ Make sure your colors are lightfast. It is best to let things wait around the studio in bright light for a month or so to see if the colors are lightfast, or fade with light. A lot of broom makers who dye also use floral dyes or chemical dyes. I have no advice for you there other than follow recipies as if it is a cotton or floral stem.

TOP LEFT: A used deep turkey frying setup makes a great DIY dye vat.

TOP RIGHT: Tampico fibers can be dyed using natural dye for the brown, and a boxed commercial dye for the pink.

THE HANDMADE BROOM

TOOLS FOR THE LONG HAUL

Well, if you've read this far, you've probably gone and done it. You're in love with the craft. The importance (for health's sake!) in having an easy-to-weave setup where you can have joy and efficiency in your days cannot be understated.

I definitely sought out these improvements after a back injury from weaving many years ago and have been doing well weaving long hours since. The first things I would look to change would be to have a tying table and an efficient way to cut the brooms. Other makers really like a broom vice for stitching as well.

My everyday setup: A comfortable chair and a tying table; a home-made stacker nearby where I sort bundles to size; and all my tools in a cup or on my work table.

GOING DEEPER IN THE CRAFT

FOR WINDING BROOMS

The first upgrade is using a tying table. Plans for a simple build are linked in the Appendix. Essentially, build a spool into the bottom of the table, and set your thread up coming from behind the table so it is pulling toward you.

Another option for winding brooms is a stand up kick winder. My dad found this one used on eBay and restored it. There are also chain drive and mechanical versions of this. I use wire on the stand up winder, mostly to make full-sized brooms with hurl. I tie any brooms with fiber cords on my tying table.

FOR STITCHING

For hand-stitching I still use the same setup I shared previously in the book. I have a vice, like the one pictured below, I just prefer using the clamps. A mechanical stitcher is also an option, but is a much larger project and commitment.

FOR CUTTING

I use a broom cutter. This is essentially a modified fodder chopper. It has an adjustable slide for the neck of the broom and works like a giant paper cutter. I have seen other folks use a floral cutter as well.

TOP LEFT: Links to stand up kick winders, like the one above, can be found with some searching! This homemade model was an eBay find that needed a new belt.

TOP RIGHT: Using the standup kickwinder is an easy and efficient way to make lots of brooms.

MIDDLE: A broom ready to flat weave in a stitching vise

BOTTOM: A broom cutter was gifted to me by Gary Glascock when he retired from broom making.

THE HANDMADE BROOM

CLOSING

Watching broom making find its way into so many people's craft practices over these last years has been a true joy. I love seeing people take up, and find joy, both in the using and in the practice of making. Happy weaving to you all; I can't wait to see where you go with the craft!

RESOURCES

OTHER BOOKS ON BROOM MAKING:
Hobbs, Karen. *Swept Away: The Vanishing Art of Broom Making*. Schiffer Crafts, 2017.

Young, William Henry. *Buy a Besom Broom: The Story of a Broom*. Treaty-Line Museum, Ind., 1976.

ON BROOMCORN:
www.uky.edu/ccd/sites/www.uky.edu.ccd/files/broomcorn.pdf

Broom-corn and Brooms: A Treatise on Raising Broom-corn and Making Brooms, on a Small or Large Scale, 1830.

Martin, John Holmes, and Washburn, Raymond Secord. *Broomcorn Growing and Handling*.

ON SHARPENING:
Hellman, Sean. *Sharp*. Crafty Little Press, 2021.

GREEN WOODWORKING:
Langsner, Drew. *Green Woodworking: a Hands on Approach*. 2nd Edition. Sterling, 1995.

COPPICING:
Krawczyk, Mark, Coppice Agroforestry: Tending Trees for Products, Profit, and Woodland, New Society Publishers, 2022

TOOLS:
Sunhouse Craft, www.sunhousecraft.com

SUPPLIES:
Caddy Supply Company, www.caddysupply.com

SOLAR KILN:
www.finewoodworking.com/2024/04/04/how-to-build-a-solar-kiln

GENERAL:
Kleon, Austin. *Steal Like an Artist: 10 Things Nobody Told You About Being Creative*. Workman Publishing Group, 2012.

INDEX

Note: page numbers in *italics* indicate projects.

awl (small), 16
axes, 76–78
    about: learning about, 76
    choosing, 76
    chopping stump and, 76–78
    sharpening, 77
    using, 76–78

binding alternatives, natural, 145
broom making, author's background and, 8
broom stitching clamp, 16
broomcorn, 18–19
    about: the hurl, 18; purchasing, 18; the stalk, 18
    additional resource, 150
    growing your own, 19
    sorting, 71
bundle size, 26

chopping stump, 76–78
clamp, broom stitching, 16
claw and holding bundles, 29
Cobwebbers, *85–97*
coppicing, 72, 150
cutting, cutter for, 149
cutting handles, 73

diagrams, visual, 112
Dohaney, Tom, 79
drawknife, 79–81
drying handles, 72

Elliot, Hunter, 136
exploring broom making
    basing off work of others, 143
    dyeing broomcorn, 146–47
    experimenting with new fibers, 144–45
    improved setup options, 148–49
    natural binding alternatives, 145
    worldwide brush fibers, 144

fibers (new), experimenting with, 144–45
floor brooms. *See also* handles; Traditional Appalachian with Broomcorn; Traditional Appalachian with Just the Hurl
    about: categories of, 9; fine tuning, 119, 133; overview of, 70; setup outline for, 86–87 (*See also specific projects*); sorting broomcorn, 71; this book and, 9

Cobwebbers, *85–97*
Hearth Sweeps, *135–39*
floor spool, 16
foot brake
    about, 22
    winding, tying jerk string and, 23
Francis, Darold, 8, 116

Garmoe, Marybeth, 49
Glascock, Gary, 13, 149
grain of wood, 74–75
green woodworking, 73, 74–75, 76, 150
growing broomcorn, 19

hand brooms
    about: bundle size, 26; categories of, 9; classic start, 27; claw and holding bundles, 29; fine tuning, 33, 41, 57, 66; setup outline for, 22 (*See also specific projects*); this book and, 9; timing note, 22
    Hawks Tails, *35–41*
    Rooster Tails, *49–57*
    Turkey Wings, *25–33*
    Whisks and Pot Scrubbers, *43–47*
    Woven Tops, *59–67*
handles.
    about: driving nail/tack into, 103; falling for pretty sticks, 73
    creating, 72–83
    cutting, 73
    drawknife and, 79–81
    drying, 72
    finding, selecting, 72–73
    finishing with polisseur, 83
    grain of wood and, 74–75
    green woodworking and, 73, 74–75, 76, 150
    killing borers, 73
    kiln drying, 73–74
    purchasing, 72
    removing bark, 73, 74
    removing knots, 76, 78, 81, 83
    shaving horses/donkeys/mules and, 79
    spokeshave and, 81–83
Hawks Tails, *35–41*
Hearth Sweeps, *135–39*
holes in handles, 103
horses, shaving, 79
hurl, about, 18. *See also* broomcorn

jerk string, 22, 23. *See also specific projects*

knives
    about: preferred types, 13
    sharpening, 14–15
    tool for sharpening, 13
knots, removing, 76, 78, 81, 83

Langsner, Drew, 74, 76

materials needed. *See* tools and materials
mules, using, 79

natural binding alternatives, 145
needle and stays, 16
new fibers, experimenting with, 144–45

pattern consideration, 62
persistence, 31
polisseur (polisher), 83
Pot Scrubbers, Whisks and, *43–47*
projects. *See* floor brooms; hand brooms

resources, other, 150
Rooster Tails, *49–57*
round, weaving in, 93–97

safety tips, 75–76, 78. *See also specific tools*
setups. *See also specific projects*
    for floor brooms, 86–87
    for hand brooms, 22
    improvements in, 148–49
sharpening tools
    about: additional resource on, 150; overview of, 13
    axes, 77
    drawknife, 80
    general guidelines, 14–15
    materials needed, 13
    sharp knives and, 13
    spokeshave, 82
    when to sharpen, 77
shaving horses/donkeys/mules, 79
shoulders and sides, 118
size of bundles, 26
sorting broomcorn, 71
spokeshave, 81–83
spool, floor, 16
stalk, about, 18. *See also* broomcorn
starting small, 131
sticks, selecting, 73
stitching setup, 149
string, jerk, 23
stump, chopping, 76–78
style, notes on, 55, 116
supplies. *See* tools and materials

tapering tips, 132
thread, 16–18
timing, handbroom creation, 22
tools and materials. *See also* broomcorn; knives; sharpening tools
    about: making your own tools, 17; overview of, 12
    awl (small), 16
    axes, 76–78
    broom stitching clamp, 16
    drawknife, 79–81
    floor spool, 16
    needle and stays, 16
    polisseur (polisher), 83
    safety tips, 75–76, 78 (*See also specific tools*)
    shaping tools (photo), 75
    spokeshave, 81–83
    thread, 16–18
    websites for, 150
Traditional Appalachian with Broomcorn, *99–119*
    about: fine tuning, 119; overview of, 99; setup, 100–101; shoulders and sides, 118; style choices, 116; visual diagram, 112
    flat weaving, 112–19
    outer layer, 108–11
    weaving, 102–7
Traditional Appalachian with Just the Hurl, *121–33*
    about: fine tuning, 133; getting comfortable with weaving tops, 131; overview of, 121; setup, 122–23; tapering stalks as you go, 132
    weaving process, 124–33
Turkey Wings, *25–33*
twilling, 64

Van Driesche, Emmet, 83
visual diagram, for flat weaving, 112

Wade, Emilie Weber, 64
weaving process. *See specific projects*
Whisks and Pot Scrubbers, *43–47*
winding brooms, upgrade for, 149
winding the foot brake, 23
wood handles. *See* handles
Woven Tops, *59–67*

MORE GREAT BOOKS *from* BLUE HILLS PRESS

The Handcarved Bowl
$27.95 | 248 Pages

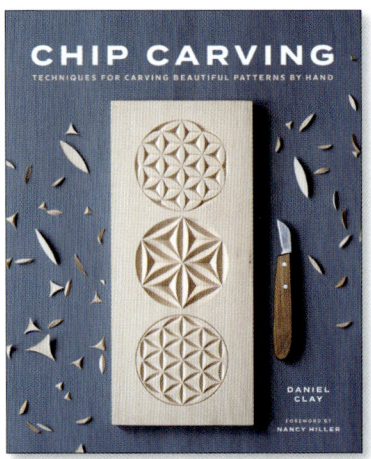

Chip Carving
$27.95 | 208 Pages

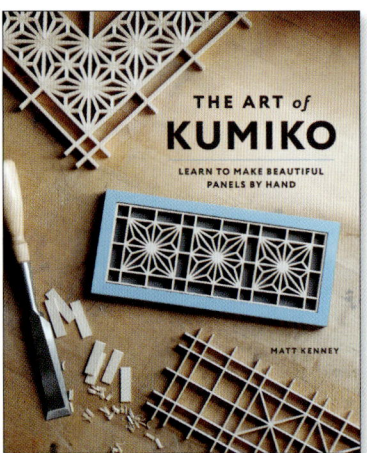

The Art of Kumiko
$27.95 | 168 Pages

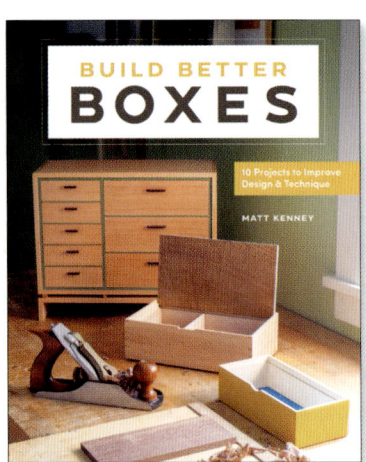

Build Better Boxes
$27.95 | 176 Pages

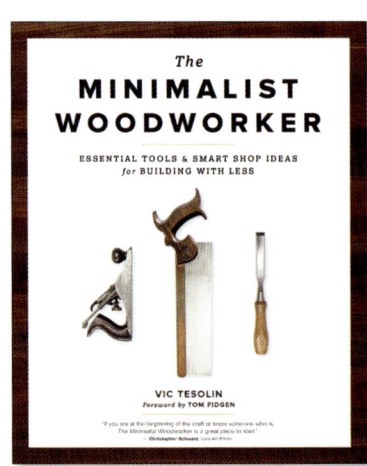

The Minimalist Woodworker
$27.95 | 152 Pages

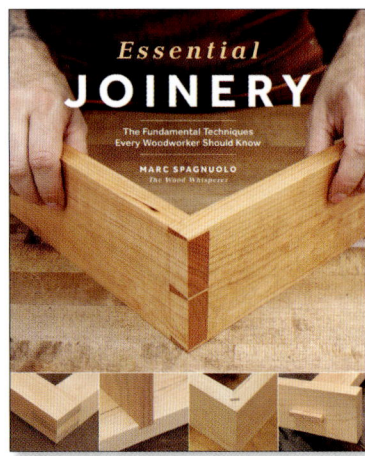

Essential Joinery
$29.95 | 216 Pages

Look for these Blue Hills Press titles at your favorite bookstore, specialty retailer, or visit *www.bluehillspress.com*.
For more information about Blue Hills Press, email us at *info@bluehillspress.com*.